T0339728

Cambridge Elements ≡

Elements in Politics and Society in Southeast Asia
edited by
Edward Aspinall
Australian National University
Meredith L. Weiss
University at Albany, SUNY

CIVIL SOCIETY IN SOUTHEAST ASIA

Power Struggles and Political Regimes

Garry Rodan
University of Queensland

CAMBRIDGE
UNIVERSITY PRESS

Shaftesbury Road, Cambridge CB2 8EA, United Kingdom

One Liberty Plaza, 20th Floor, New York, NY 10006, USA

477 Williamstown Road, Port Melbourne, VIC 3207, Australia

314–321, 3rd Floor, Plot 3, Splendor Forum, Jasola District Centre,
New Delhi – 110025, India

103 Penang Road, #05–06/07, Visioncrest Commercial, Singapore 238467

Cambridge University Press is part of Cambridge University Press & Assessment,
a department of the University of Cambridge.

We share the University's mission to contribute to society through the pursuit of
education, learning and research at the highest international levels of excellence.

www.cambridge.org
Information on this title: www.cambridge.org/9781108707428

DOI: 10.1017/9781108757423

First published 2022

A catalogue record for this publication is available from the British Library.

ISBN 978-1-108-70742-8 Paperback
ISSN 2515-2998 (online)
ISSN 2515-298X (print)

Civil Society in Southeast Asia

Power Struggles and Political Regimes

Elements in Politics and Society in Southeast Asia

DOI: 10.1017/9781108757423
First published online: September 2022

Garry Rodan
University of Queensland

Author for correspondence: Garry Rodan, g.rodan@uq.edu.au

Abstract: Contrary to popular claims, civil society is not generally shrinking in Southeast Asia. It is transforming, resulting in important shifts in the influences that can be exerted through it. Political and ideological differences in Southeast Asia have sharpened as anti-democratic and anti-liberal social forces compete with democratic and liberal elements in civil society. These are neither contests between civil society and uncivil society nor a tussle between civil society and state power. They are power struggles over relationships between civil society and the state. Explaining these struggles, the approach in this Element emphasises the historical and political economy foundations shaping conflicts, interests, and coalitions that mobilise through civil society. Different ways that capitalism is organised, controlled, and developed are shown to matter for when, how, and in what direction conflicts in civil society emerge and coalitions form. This argument is demonstrated through comparisons of Singapore, Malaysia, the Philippines, and Thailand.

Keywords: civil society, capitalism, ideology, democratisation, authoritarianism

ISBNs: 9781108707428 (PB), 9781108757423 (OC)
ISSNs: 2515-2998 (online), 2515-298X (print)

Contents

1 Theorising Civil Society

It is impossible to comprehend the character and direction of any political regime without understanding the extent and nature of civil society. After all, civil society is a distinct collective political space that is legally supported by the state, but also offers the most substantive capacity and potential for social forces to resist and cooperate with the state in their own interests (Rodan 1997: 158).

According to Toepler and colleagues (2020: 649), democrats therefore have plenty to be concerned about. They refer to literature contending a general shrinking of the space of civil society 'amid the growth of hybrid and authoritarian regimes worldwide'. Some academic and popular writers go so far as to claim that civil society – and, hence, democracy – faces growing challenges from forces and mobilisations constituting a contending *uncivil society* (see Ruzza 2009; Harrington 2019, for example).

However, these conceptualisations and arguments conceal as much as they reveal. The political space of civil society has been in decline in some regimes, with authoritarian politics making significant gains over the last decade or more. Yet profound political changes to civil society and political regimes also elude mainstream analysts – a problem that this study of Southeast Asia attempts to address. Indeed, *this study does not so much discern a general shrinking of civil society space but important shifts in the influences exerted through it*. Both democratic and anti-democratic ideologies and forces are integral to these struggles for influence.

Literature on Southeast Asia has hitherto been dominated by two – often implicit – questions. First, how has civil society shaped or enabled forces and groups seeking increased political openness? Second, how have civil society–state relations been obstructed or shaped by powerful elites? The findings here arise from adopting a framework that is geared instead towards answering questions of *how* and *why* spaces for contestation and reform differ from one country to another.

In Southeast Asia and other capitalist societies, civil society is the locus of inequalities based on class, but also on ethnicity, gender, race, sexuality, and other symptoms of specific social and political systems of power underpinned by the state (Wood 1990). Many inequalities therefore predate capitalism. Yet the conditions under which struggles over them are conducted – and the possible coalitions forming in those struggles – are also fundamentally influenced by the transformative, conflictual, and contradictory nature of contemporary capitalism. Consequently, analysis that fails to theorise civil society's relationship to capitalist development is incomplete.

From the 1960s, capitalist development and Cold War geopolitics combined in Southeast Asia to foster powerful new ruling classes (Glassman 2018). State repression in this period broadly dismantled or seriously weakened independent class-based and many other independent organisations. Cohesive, influential, and sustainable mass civil society movements or coalitions – especially socialist and social democratic ones – proved difficult to rebuild or establish following the Cold War's end. Beginning in the 1980s, structural pressures emanating from advancing economic globalisation also militated against strong, independent trade unions (Hutchison and Brown 2001).

Yet, paradoxically, the taming of civil society laid foundations for elites to embark on varying neoliberal capitalist reforms across the region, generating social structural changes fuelling new conflicts over state power and accentuating existing ones. Technocratic liberal reformist framings of conflict – let alone other more democratic framings – have faced concerted challenges, including from religious, ethnic, cultural, and nationalist depictions of the causes of, and solutions to, conflict (Jayasuriya and Rodan 2007; Jayasuriya 2020).

As elsewhere in the world, many of these ideological variations of identity politics are resonating with elements of middle classes now confronted with more precarious employment, rising living costs, and other pressures generated by neoliberal capitalism and market values. Hence, precisely as rising inequality under capitalism intensifies, cross-class civil society alliances to tackle systemic inequality are becoming less – not more – likely. It is against this background that assorted anti-liberal and anti-democratic civil society mobilisations surfaced in the last decade in Southeast Asia. This ranges from the royalist Yellow Shirt movement in Thailand and ethnic nationalist and religious nationalist movements in Indonesia, Myanmar, and Malaysia, to support for human rights abuses in the Philippines in the so-called war on drugs under authoritarian President Duterte.

Meanwhile, civil society coalitions in Malaysia were pivotal in mobilising to bring down the authoritarian Prime Minister Najib Razak and his *Barisan Nasional* (*BN*, or National Front) in 2018 – the first change of government since the country's political independence in 1957. However, as in earlier civil society mobilisations helping to remove authoritarian leaders Marcos in the Philippines and Soeharto in Indonesia, a change of government in Malaysia where forces in civil society played crucial roles marked a new phase – not the end – in the struggle over state power. Hence, the new government – *Pakatan Harapan* (*PH*, or Coalition of Hope) – collapsed within two years amidst internal friction.

Clearly, understanding which interests and ideologies are harnessed through civil society – and to what end – is indispensable to explaining where political regimes in Southeast Asia are headed and why.

Towards that understanding, a distinctive political economy framework of analysis is adopted here that emphasises civil society contestation *over* state power relationships in civil society rather than a struggle *between* civil society and state; civil society as a political space open to democratic, non-democratic, and anti-democratic forces and ideologies; ideology as pivotal in *mediating* civil society struggles over state power; and the importance of historical specificity in how capitalism is organised and controlled for explaining variations in civil society conflicts and coalitions across countries.

The different elements of this framework cohere to mount the argument that civil society in Southeast Asia is transformed through its changing relationships to state power and struggles thereof. Such an argument is only possible, though, by transcending liberal notions of civil society and state and how these relate to political regime dynamics.

Some liberal theorists continue to adopt highly normatively positive conceptions of civil society as primarily a *counter* to the power of the state and lament the advent of uncivil society. Others acknowledge some power ambiguities, notably that the state protects the political independence of civil society, also conceding that civil society can house undemocratic elements. Nevertheless, here civil society and state remain analytically separated in ways that obscure links between politics and social class that shape power struggles over political regimes.

Consequently, there remains no liberal framework for adequately explaining how, when, and why civil society serves as a realm through which activists shape state power to either enhance, consolidate, or reduce the interests and positions of particular social groups. Weberian models of ideal typical institutions to scrutinise political and state bureaucratic institutions – influential in the literature on Southeast Asia – fall well short of conceptualising or explaining such political interrelationships.

The framework here draws on Gramsci (1971), who emphasised the artificiality of the distinction between civil society and state under capitalism, highlighting patterned power differentials between different social classes reinforced across these seemingly separate political spheres. Civil society assumes broader meaning than the independent collective organisations and associations emphasised by liberal theorists. It incorporates a set of social structures and, crucially, constitutes a site of ideological struggle over whether or not persistent unequal social, political, and economic relationships are subject to scrutiny and political mobilisation (Gramsci 1971: 12; see also Anderson 1976).

Collective political organisations and movements within civil society may thus be technically independent of the state, but their actions are integral to defining and expressing state power.

Southeast Asia offers a fascinating empirical focus for demonstrating the general theoretical utility of understanding the inseparability of state and civil society. Stunning economic and social transformations in the last fifty years in the region have combined with a diverse range of authoritarian and democratic political regime directions, many of which remain seriously contested. Explaining the varying extents and complexions of civil society and their political significance for state power is thus no small challenge – but an ideal one for general theoretical purposes.

Before embarking on the case studies, though, the intellectual histories and geopolitical contexts that have shaped competing ideas about civil society and state within Southeast Asia are examined. This provides foundations for distinguishing the core concepts and definitions of the framework introduced in Section 1.4. This framework will guide the case studies of civil society in Singapore, Malaysia, the Philippines, and Thailand.

1.1 A History of Civil Society

Modern notions of civil society started to emerge with eighteenth-century struggles in Western Europe to dismantle the absolutist state and affect a transition from feudalism to capitalism (Brook 1997: 19–20). Then, and subsequently, the meaning and purpose of civil society have varied, and its influence has waxed and waned among scholars and policymakers. Positive normative assumptions about civil society are, however, a striking theme, many writers routinely championing the liberalising and democratising significance of civil society. Such contributions are not without insights, but they cannot adequately conceptualise or explain the inherently conflictual nature of civil society as a site of political contestation over the exercise of state power.

It was in the context of the European transition to capitalism and the accompanying Age of Enlightenment that the civil society concept was explicitly adopted. This was the time when, Bernhard (1993: 308) writes, civil society first began to take shape as an 'historical phenomenon', when 'social groups were emancipated from restrictions placed on them by feudal and absolutist systems'. More substantial challenges to monarchical power followed from the bourgeoisie. In the process, a sphere of autonomy for social actors sprang up 'between the official public life of the monarchy, the state and the nobility, and that of private and/or communal life' (Bernhard 1993: 308).

More generally, Enlightenment thinkers prosecuted the claim that rational human beings could determine their own destiny without subordination to absolute state control (Laine 2014: 62). By contrast, Marx equated civil society with 'bourgeois society', rejecting claims that the struggle against the absolutist state was about the universal rights of people and citizens, rather than the particular interests of the bourgeoisie in the 'ruthless logic of commodity production and exchange' (Keane 2005: 25).

While not explicitly adopting the term civil society, in the first half of the eighteenth century, French liberal theorist Tocqueville also argued the vital importance of diverse civil associations to representative democracy's success in America – curbing despotism by limiting the scope and power of government (Keane 1999: 309). According to Tocqueville (in Stid 2018): 'In democratic countries, the knowledge of how to form associations is the mother of all knowledge since the success of all the others depends on it'.

Such public space expanded in Europe to encompass a diverse range of professional and non-professional associations, organisations (including independent press and publishers), and political parties. Yet the struggle to establish new political regimes was a protracted and fractious one. Attempts through civil society to advance politically inclusive and egalitarian agendas, notably via working-class-controlled organisations, were critical to the realisation of various forms of liberal democracy in much of Europe and the United Kingdom and their consolidation in the twentieth century. As Eley (2002) points out, though, agendas of social and political inclusivity were – and remain – subject to resistance from other elements of civil society.

Collective organisation also emerged in Southeast Asia that enjoyed periodic influence, reflecting 'European streams of thought' (Du Bois 1962: 42–4). Labour organisations grew in the 1920s and were boosted by the advent of the 1930 Great Depression. By the late 1930s, communist and socialist movements emerged, linked and divided by ethnicity and shaped by nationalist, anti-colonial, and anti-imperialist movements. Nationalism was the dynamic force in the 1940s and 1950s in challenges to colonialism. Most socialists had adopted anti-communist stances by the 1950s, but they were also opposed to capitalism due to its links with colonialism (Hewison and Rodan 1994: 240–7).

For much of the twentieth century, though, the rise of authoritarian states through fascism, communism, and the Cold War delivered blows to civil societies in many parts of the world, not least in Southeast Asia (see Hewison and Rodan 1994; Hansson, Hewison, and Glassman 2020). Theorisation of civil society thus lacked the political immediacy and the degree of analytical appeal among scholars it previously enjoyed. This changed from the 1970s when civil societies played important roles in movements in Latin America, Asia, and Eastern Europe in the downfall of authoritarian regimes.

Thematic to civil society's resurgence in academic and policy influence was a pervasive normative embrace of civil society as the ingredient needed to build, rebuild, or replenish democratic politics. Scholars wanted to understand how it was that seemingly monolithic and oppressive regimes were brought to heel, and how to consolidate and extend the political power of non-state actors in post-authoritarian societies. The economic, social, and political decay and crises of the Soviet Union by the late 1980s, leading to its dissolution and the end of the Cold War by 1991, provided further impetus for civil society's intellectual revival.

Against this background, Fukuyama's (1989: 4) influential 'end of history' thesis was born, according to which 'mankind's ideological evolution and the universalization of Western liberal democracy as the final form of human government' was imminent. Huntington (1991) also linked capitalist globalisation to a 'Third Wave' of democratisations, reviving earlier modernisation theory's notion that liberal politics and economics were natural, functional partners. Such arguments heightened expectations of democratisation and associated civil society expansion in Southeast Asia and elsewhere.

There was also renewed interest in the role and significance of associational life in established liberal democracies, Putnam's works on Italy (1993) and America (1995) being particularly influential. His emphasis on social capital – as avenues for civic participation, associated shared values, and resultant mutual trust among citizens in each other and their institutions – was taken up by the World Bank and a raft of other multilateral agencies, non-governmental organisations (NGOs), and academics championing civil society (Carothers 2004). Programmes to build civil society 'capacity' and 'social capital' became integral to foreign aid strategies for economic and social development, including in Southeast Asia (Carroll 2010). Transnational civil society networks also expanded in attempts to influence a wide range of decision-making processes (Florini 2000).

This intellectual and policy resurgence of civil society was, as Viterna, Clough, and Clarke (2015: 181) observe, considered intrinsically positive, since 'civil society organizations [CSOs] protected human rights, promoted solidarity, and represented the true interests of the people, not the powerful'. However, a proliferation of professional CSOs around the globe from the 1990s often supplanted, or reduced the influence of, organisational members (Skocpol 2004; Edwards 2011).[1] Rueschemeyer and colleagues (1992: 49) also argued that where 'powerful and cohesive upper classes' dominate CSOs, they can 'serve as conduits of authoritarian ideologies, thus weakening democracy'. Keane (2005: 27) contended that 'market presumptions' had structurally and ideologically penetrated the thinking and operations of many CSOs.

---

[1] CSOs refers in this Element to all independent organisations acting politically, including NGOs and POs.

Furthermore, often lurking behind seemingly progressive rhetoric from CSO actors about accountability and representation are non-democratic and anti-democratic ideological assumptions and claims. This includes moral ideologies of accountability grounded in traditional sources of authority – such as monarchs and religious leaders – or in charismatic figures who act as moral guardians to interpret or ordain correct codes of behaviour for public officials (Rodan and Hughes 2014). It also includes ideologies of representation and participation privileging technocratic notions of problem-solving and consensus ahead of competing definitions of, and solutions to, policy problems (Jayasuriya and Rodan 2007; Rodan 2018).

Indeed, it transpired that liberal optimism about an end of history was misplaced. Not too long into the twenty-first century, democratic transitions theorists began lamenting a global trend towards 'democratic backsliding' (Waldner and Lust 2018) and the worldwide 'shrinking or closing space for civil society' (Toepler et al. 2020: 649).

In Southeast Asia, authoritarian politics has become increasingly evident in the last decade, compounded by the advent of the COVID-19 pandemic (Kurlantzick 2020). Such a juncture – not unique to this region – calls into question the adequacy of influential theoretical concepts and frameworks for understanding civil society directions.

1.2 Virtuous Civil Society

Conceptions of civil society that give approving emphasis to civility, liberty, plurality, independence, and voluntary associations remain influential. These themes are often equated with liberal democracy itself. However, civil society is a contested political space, through which struggles can be conducted not just *for* democracy but also *over* democracy and even *against* democracy.

Differences abound in the ways that civil society has been conceived by theorists (see Ehrenberg 1999; Keane 1999; Edwards 2020). Of special interest here, though, is what politics qualify for, or are excluded from, notions of civil society.

Some liberal notions of civil society portray it as a residual category – the realm of social relations outside state or market. Walzer (1991: 293), for example, understood civil society as 'the space of uncoerced human association' involving 'groups of all sorts, not for the sake of any particular formation – family, tribe, nation, religion, commune, brotherhood or sisterhood, interest group or ideological movement – but for the sake of sociability itself. For we are by nature social, before we are political or economic beings' (Walzer 1991: 298). Mirsky (1993: 572) described civil society as 'a social sphere in which no single locus of authority predominates and in which men and women interact with each other in a series of overlapping relationships and associations – communal, civic, religious, economic, social, and cultural'.

However, the concept of civil society must be preserved for specifying a particular form of *political* space.[2] The aim of activists – if not always the outcome – is to influence the exercise of state power. As Ehrenberg (1999: 235–6) observed, understanding civil society 'as a nonmarket, nonstate sphere of voluntary activity is not enough to help us make crucial distinctions between Putnam's bowling leagues, soccer teams, and choral societies on the one hand, and Greenpeace, the National Organization for Women, and the Ku Klux Klan on the other'.

Among the many liberal theorists who accept this distinction, there is a wealth of statements about, and endorsements of, the political nature of civil society. Diamond (2016) provides a particularly clear contemporary example of such: 'the *realm of organized social life that is voluntary, self-regulating, (largely) self-supporting, autonomous from the state, and bound by a legal order or set of shared rules.* [emphasis in original] ... an intermediary entity, standing between the private sphere and the state ... [that] encompasses "the ideological marketplace" and the flow of information and ideas' (119–20).

Yet, while Diamond (2016: 120) considers civil society as intrinsically political, he draws the line at attempts by civic organisations and movements to secure formal political power or office in the state, or to change the nature of the state 'from a desire to capture state power for the group per se'. This does not rule out engagement with political parties to achieve reforms, but parties per se are not considered part of civil society. After all, the point of civil society for liberals is principally to counter state power and hold it to account.

Rosenblum (2000: 500–1) challenges the 'moral valence' many theorists attach to voluntary civil society associations vis-à-vis parties. Indeed, she considers parties the preeminent 'strong republics' when their deliberative nature is exercised. The important normative question, then, is over 'the extent to which party agendas are the substantive outcome of deliberation among a broad and active membership' (Rosenblum 2000: 528). Where analytical focus is less on a sharp delineation of state and civil society, and more on the interrelationship between one and the other – as is the case here – the argument for distinguishing parties from other intermediary organisations is not compelling. Indeed, Gramsci's conception of civil society incorporates political parties (Alagappa 2004: 29).

---

[2] For examples of the different ways the concept of political space has been applied to Asia, see Hansson and Weiss (2018).

However, this cannot mean linking of parties and other organisations through civil society is axiomatic or definitional. Civil societies can involve varying relationships between their formal (party) and informal (non-party) elements – both of which are political.[3] These boundaries can and do change. Historically specific patterns of capitalist development, and the dynamics thereof, are crucial to explaining such shifting configurations of civil society, including the boundaries between formal and informal civil society.

In Southeast Asia, Cold War repression and new strategies of capitalist development hostile to independent labour resulted in the dismantling of radical trade unions and other organisations, while parties linked to them faced intimidation or bans.[4] Under tighter political limits and with expanded middle classes, different civil societies emerged in a shift from radical to bourgeois opposition and reform advocacy (Hewison and Rodan 2012). The precise extent and nature of political connections through civil society continue to unfold in varying ways across the region.

Variations stem not simply from the region comprising one-party, or one-party dominant, political systems and others with more competitive systems. These are *outcomes* – not underlying *drivers* – of shifting boundaries between the formal and informal political spaces of civil society.

The People's Action Party (PAP) in Singapore, for example, transformed from a grassroots party organically linking formal and informal political elements to a top-down party. This was the result of a struggle over state power between competing factions with different plans for Singapore's capitalist development in which technocratic authoritarians triumphed. By contrast, in authoritarian Malaysia, the United Malays National Organisation (UMNO) did not take this technocratic path, and boundaries between formal and informal civil society are in greater flux.

Some political economies are, at a certain historical juncture, more conducive to coalitions through formal and informal civil society spaces than others, regardless of regime type, as the case studies will highlight. What matters most for regime directions is not whether coalitions constitute some ideal typical configuration of civil society, but the scale and direction of opposition and/or reform that can be pursued through this political space.

Civil society is also distinguished in Diamond's (2016: 120) account by civility and political pluralism: when an organisation aims 'to monopolize a functional or political space in society, claiming that it represents the only

---

[3] Hence, preference here for 'formal civil society' and 'informal civil society' over terms of 'civil society' and 'political society' to distinguish the same elements.

[4] See Hicken and Kuhonta (2015) for analyses of institutional constraints on political parties in Southeast Asia.

legitimate path, it contradicts the pluralistic and market-oriented nature of civil society'. This point speaks as much to the culture of civil society as it does to its associational forms, something that early modernisation theorists Almond and Verba (1963) gave particular emphasis to as a prerequisite for democracy (see also Putnam 1993, 2000).

Emphasis on civility can also be found across critical, post-structuralist, and postmodernist notions of civil society. Enlightenment values emphasising reason and rationality have been influential in fostering emphasis on the cooperative and/or problem-solving virtues of civil society (Cohen and Arato 1992: 71–80; Huang 1993: 218–19). Thus, while preferred models of democracy differ between theoretical camps, Aspinall's (2004: 90) claim that 'only a democratic civil society that is truly *civil* supports democracy' has general resonance across the literature.

Yet recent proliferation of organisations and mobilisations departing from the political values or conduct prescribed above has led to authors across theoretical camps emphasising differences between *civil* society and *uncivil* society. This distinction can hinder a full grasp of the contested nature of civil society in the struggle over state power.

Violent and/or unconstitutional behaviour has long been viewed as antithetical to any notion of civil society. In recent decades, though, cultural values have become an additional point of distinction. Ruzza (2009: 87) defines *uncivil* society as an historically located 'set of associational activities characterized by discursively exclusionist, undemocratic or violent features'. Organisational activities and worldviews of this ilk include those that are 'racist, nationalist and populist, and characterized as biologically essentialist, or territorially or culturally exclusionist' (Ruzza 2009: 87).

Nearly two decades ago, Kopecký and Mudde (2003) rightly raised concerns about the vague boundaries between *civil* and *uncivil* society. They also argued against separating either 'uncivil movements' or 'contentious politics' from the study of civil society – especially in dynamic post-authoritarian or fledgling democracies. Platek and Plucienniczak (2016: 4) subsequently pointed to how elements of far-right movements in Poland shifted within a decade from extreme positions occupied in the 1990s.

The continued attraction of the concept of 'uncivil' society reflects the normative power of the prevailing neo-Tocquevillian and other romantic liberal notions of civil society rejected here. This is despite the observation by Berman (1997: 401), from a competing liberal theoretical camp, that a 'robust civil society actually helped scuttle the twentieth century's most critical democratic experiment, Weimar Germany', paving the path for fascism (see also Armony 2004).

In short, if we define away all forces and values hostile to democracy – even where they act in a constitutional and non-violent manner – we limit our capacity to comprehend some of the most significant political associations and ideologies engaged in struggles to reshape and/or defend existing state power relationships in contemporary Southeast Asia – and elsewhere.

Importantly, there is growing literature eschewing the concept of 'uncivil society', or adopting it in qualified ways, including authors from the liberal tradition. This work is empirically rich in its attempts to identify and discern different non-democratic and anti-democratic elements within civil society movements (see Youngs 2018, for example).

Thus, while the concept of 'uncivil society' continues to enjoy currency in literature on Southeast Asia (see Kingston 2020, for example), other works have emerged examining forces and ideologies of ethnic, religious, and royalist nationalism operating in civil society (see, e.g. Janjira 2018, 2021; Wilson 2019; Aspinall et al. 2020; Lorch 2021; Mietzner 2021). Complementary studies focus on the harnessing of social media technologies across the region to advance a range of anti-democratic forces and ideologies through civil society (see, e.g. Paladino 2018; Sinpeng 2021; Weiss 2021).

These interventions, some of which are incorporated into this study, further highlight the limitations of the neo-Tocquevillian understanding of civil societies in Southeast Asia. However, the exercise here is more ambitious – not only to decisively transcend the democratic transitions problematic but also to expose the limitations of Diamond's (2016: 120) notion of civil societies as intrinsically 'pluralistic and market oriented'. Neither such conditions infer an equal ability among different civil society actors to influence state power – whether 'civility' is observed or not.

Such ability is a function of power relations *within* and *between* civil society and state, to which we now turn. We need to look beyond liberal theory to adequately conceptualise and explain these dynamic power relations – and important shifts in the influences over state power resulting in Southeast Asia.

1.3 Civil Society–State Relations

Challenges to democracy and support for authoritarianism in established liberal democracies, and those thought to be emerging or prospective ones, have increasingly fuelled greater consideration of the complex interrelations between state and civil society. However, important differences exist over whether analytical frameworks transcend or reinforce the democratic transitions problematic and related state–civil society dichotomy, and over the degrees and ways that capitalism is analytically incorporated.

Reconsideration of the relationship between civil society and state by liberal theorists has included more comprehensive scrutiny of political institutions. Much analysis centres on so-called hybrid regimes, thought to have institutional elements of a democracy, but whose democratic quality is compromised (see, e.g. Diamond 2002; Levitsky and Way 2010). This approach is well represented in the literature on Southeast Asia (see, e.g. Case 2002; Morlino, Dressel, and Pelizzo 2011). Many such regimes are portrayed as experiencing 'democratic backsliding', defined by Bermeo (2016: 16) as 'the weakening or disassembling of *a given set* of democratic institutions' [italics in original]. Analyses of 'backsliding' in Southeast Asia are rapidly expanding (see, e.g. Aspinall et al. 2020; Croissant and Haynes 2021; Mietzner 2021).

Explicitly, or implicitly, many such works evaluate institutional practices and performances against benchmarks of liberal-democratic ideal types, sometimes extending to Weberian critiques of state forms where patrimonialism is present.[5] Liberal theoretical frameworks dominating this literature evaluate a plurality of factors or variables considered relevant to democratic institutional integrity, one of which is *active* civil society (Bermeo 2016: 15).

However, civil society activism can be no less important to overthrowing democratically elected governments as it can unelected dictators. Civil society is a site of struggle over whose interests and ideologies prevail in the exercise of state power. Institutions are not separate from this struggle but embody and reflect it. Concerns here are thus more fundamental compared to the above literature: to explain the coalitions both *for* and *against* democracy and how they become rooted in civil society. To do this we must establish what social structures are to be linked to the formation of political coalitions shaping civil society and state relationships, and how.

A broad distinction can be drawn between varieties of liberal pluralist and Marxist-influenced class approaches. The former incorporates socio-economic factors and variables into analyses of different interest and pressure groups competing and cooperating in civil society to counter or cooperate with state power. The latter thematically emphasises dynamic class relationships under capitalism as fundamental in shaping the context of civil society struggles and the interests at stake over state power.

In the Marxist-influenced approach here, the state is understood not simply in terms of a set of functions, or a group of actors, as in Weberian theory. The state does comprise institutions through which laws, rules, and policies are enacted by officials. However, what defines the nature and character of any state is

---

[5] Morgenbesser (2019) creatively superimposed this benchmarking logic onto authoritarian regimes in Southeast Asia.

a particular set of power relations. These relations are a manifestation of the coalescence and organisation of specific social, political, ideological, and economic forces and interests (Hewison, Rodan, Robison 1993). This helps explain why institutions – be they electoral, legal, or regulatory – can be harnessed to varying political ends or abolished altogether.

This approach can identify and explain different ways that relationships between civil society and state power are playing out across Southeast Asia. The transformative and conflictual nature of capitalist development not only exerts pressures towards social and economic inequalities but also lays foundations for *potential* new coalitions of social and political forces seeking to challenge or consolidate institutional limits to political conflict. This potential is, however, *mediated* by ideology. How capitalism is organised and controlled differs from one country to another, thus the precise interests, conflicts, and contradictions setting the context for struggles and coalitions of material and ideological interest over state power necessarily varies across Southeast Asia.

Emphasis on capitalist dynamics does not deny the importance of social cleavages beyond class. On the contrary, the approach here draws heavily on Gramsci's characterisation of civil society as an arena of ideological and cultural contestation encompassing a diverse range of identities and values. It was precisely the failure of revolutionary class consciousness to emerge out of capitalist transformations in the twentieth century in Europe that led Gramsci to part company with Marx on the understanding of civil society–state relationships. Yet Gramsci's emphasis on ideational power was meant to supplement – not replace – analysis of structural power relationships rooted in class.

For Gramsci, civil society is necessarily a relationship between dominant and dominated classes, the former enjoying ideological hegemony when it succeeds in 'attempts to exercise its political, moral, and intellectual leadership to establish its view of the world as all-inclusive and universal, and to shape the interests of subordinate groups' (Carnoy 1984: 70). His analytical focus thus extended to the roles of a wide assortment of organisations and associations, including schools, churches, and cultural bodies integral to the generation of worldviews benefitting a 'dominant' or 'historic' bloc of social forces.

Gramsci's notion of civil society as a realm of *contestation* has proven attractive to a range of scholars. Yet, as Lorch (2021: 82) observes, 'neo-Gramscians often view civil society positively as an arena of counter-hegemonic struggle' but have been less concerned with 'the hegemony of the (bourgeois) ruling class over civil society'. This observation rings true of literature on Southeast Asia primarily analysing ideational power (see, e.g. Landau 2008; O'Shannassy 2008; Chong 2010; Teo 2019). Such work is a significant advance on neo-Tocquevillian approaches. However, it also reflects a false separation, as if discursive struggles over state power can be disentangled from class interests.

Departures from this false separation include books by Hilley (2001) and Hedman (2006), respectively, on Malaysia and the Philippines, and articles on Thailand by Glassman (2011) and on Singapore by Tan (2012). These Gramscian accounts of hegemonic domination, and attempted challenges to it, analytically integrate structural (class) relationships and ideational aspects of civil society contestation over state power. This enabled these writers to offer persuasive explanations for the historic timing and outcomes of intensified civil society struggles over state power, insights which will be drawn in the four case studies of civil society struggles in Singapore, Malaysia, the Philippines, and Thailand.

Integrated analysis of capitalist class dynamics and ideological battles is thus necessary for answering the question of how and why contestation through civil society differs from one country in Southeast Asia to another. We must also be able to identify and analyse competing ideas and support bases, not just for democracy, but also for non-democratic alternatives, within and across different political regimes. This is the purpose of the modes of participation (MOP) framework, elements of which have been inferred in Sections 1.2 and 1.3 but whose concepts are now specified in Section 1.4.

1.4 Modes of Participation Framework

To reiterate, the political significance of civil society is a function of power relations *within* and *between* civil society and state. Accordingly, the MOP framework contributes distinctive conceptualisations to analyse struggles over civil society–state relationships and other political spaces through which contestation may be channelled. A MOP refers to the institutional arrangements and accompanying ideological rationales defining the permissible limits to who can politically participate, how and on what basis. Some MOPs may support substantive challenges to deeply entrenched power relations, while others facilitate participation protecting those relationships.[6]

There are four MOPs institutionally managing political conflict. *Civil society expression* through independently created forms of collective action involves most relative political autonomy from state regulatory control. It thus represents the greatest potential threat – and support – to existing state political control and associated interests. Political parties and a diverse range of organisations, pressure, and interest groups through to mass movements

---

[6] This framework is outlined in much greater detail in Jayasuriya and Rodan (2007) and Rodan (2018).

that might have revolutionary aims and *modus operandi* belong to this MOP. *Individualised expression* enjoys a similar degree of relative political autonomy from the state and includes engagement with a member of parliament (MP), petition signing, talkback radio calls, political cartoons, and blog sites (Rodan 2018: 34–6).

In sharp contrast, through *societal incorporation*, state- or trans-state-sponsored institutions provide avenues through which groups may influence public policy, yet on terms set by officials. Some activists engage with this MOP tactically to pursue more ambitious agendas than officially intended (Jayasuriya and Rodan 2007: 783). Individuals can also be steered to institutions of *administrative incorporation* including public grievance, consultation, and feedback mechanisms of state bureaucracies. Here conflicts are translated into issues about the refinement and implementation of government policy.

The framework also introduces non-democratic ideologies of political representation and participation – *consultative* and *particularist* – alongside the more established concepts of *democratic* and *populist* ideologies. As with the MOPs, these four ideologies are not strictly mutually exclusive, but fundamentally differ in emphasis – with important implications for preferred state–civil society power relationships.

Primary emphasis in *democratic* ideologies is on actors being directly or indirectly accountable to fellow citizens. Representation is also a means by which political conflict and competition is conducted, intrinsic to which are intermediary groups in civil society (Pitkin 1967). *Populist* ideologies emphasise direct links between 'the people' and the leadership of a political movement (Laclau 2007), quite often in claims of 'direct democracy' bypassing intermediary groups in a struggle against elites in general (Mouzelis 1985).

By contrast, *consultative* ideologies emphasise the problem-solving utility of incorporating stakeholders, interests, and/or expertise into the processes of public policymaking in order that the most effective functioning of social, economic, or political governance can be delivered. *Particularist* ideologies emphasise the rights to representation of discrete communities and identities variously based on race, ethnicity, religion, gender, geography, and culture. These ideologies can be used to claim and rationalise representation by either marginalised or dominant groups.

Consultative and particularist ideologies have proven attractive for state elites in strategies to pre-empt class-based or cohesive cross-class coalitions and/or multi-ethnic reformist movements – especially in the context of rising conflicts generated by the social contradictions of capitalism.

The utility of these conceptual tools will be demonstrated below through analyses of civil society in Singapore, Malaysia, the Philippines, and Thailand – cases encompassing varying models of capitalist development. Configurations of MOPs and ideologies of political participation supportive of existing state power relations differ across these models:

- Under technocratic state capitalism in Singapore, new MOPs of societal incorporation are the most extensive in Southeast Asia and central to PAP attempts to contain or counter conflict channelled through civil society expression. Consultative ideologies of political participation – often in articulation with particularist ideologies of ethnicity – are pivotal to this strategy.
- Under racialised state capitalism in Malaysia, particularist ideologies of race, ethnicity, and religion dominate elite strategies to limit contestation over state power through civil society expression.
- Under oligarchic capitalism in the Philippines, private business interests are deeply integrated with state power, undermining democratic institutions and stymying reform. Thus, periodically, societal incorporation and consensus ideologies emerge, as do populist ideologies – as alternatives or adjuncts to democratic institutions and ideologies.
- Under monarchical/military state capitalism in Thailand, state power relations benefitting these interests are rationalised by particularist ideologies of royal and religious nationalism through both civil society expression and societal incorporation.

The case studies illustrate and explain when, why, and by whom MOPs and attendant ideologies preferred by established elites are contested or supported through civil society.

Analyses here do more than empirically build on earlier applications of the MOP framework. They constitute the most integrated attempt through the framework to demonstrate the analytical inseparability of civil society and state incorporating both formal (party) and informal (societal) politics in Southeast Asia. Explaining when, why, and how coalitions across formal and informal political spaces of civil society emerge to reform or shore up existing state power relations is a thematic analytical concern here. Crucially, as the cases of Thailand and Malaysia will highlight, this can involve coalitions of democratic or authoritarian forces and ideologies – and sometimes elements of both.

Examinations of Singapore and Malaysia are a little lengthier to show the analytical depth of the framework, supplemented by more selective but still substantial demonstrations of the framework's power through the Philippines and Thai cases.

2 Technocratic State Capitalism and Civil Society Timidity in Singapore

Singapore emphatically debunks any residual myths associated with modernisation theory: it has the most advanced capitalist economy in Southeast Asia and is among the countries with the least political space of civil society. This is not because capitalist development in the city-state has been less prone to conflict than elsewhere. On the contrary, since the 1980s, Singapore's accelerated capitalist development has increasingly generated conflict over its uneven economic, social, and environmental impacts. However, this has led to the region's most extensive range of new MOPs through which to channel, contain, and respond to conflict. Meanwhile, civil society has been intricately regulated to foster groups supportive of regime interests and ideologies and constrain those who oppose or criticise them.

Indeed, of the four countries in this study, it is in Singapore under technocratic state capitalism where state–civil society power relationships are most systematically stacked against reformist forces in civil society. The political and ideological cohesion of the ruling party and de facto one-party state under this model of capitalism has made it difficult for social forces to forge bases and coalitions in civil society to engage in contestation over state power.

Social forces seeking to operate through civil society expression are limited to opposition parties mainly supported by the working class and to select NGOs led by middle-class professionals. These forces are sharply segregated, legally prevented from forming coalitions across formal and informal political spaces of civil society. They face a plethora of other constraints on collective political mobilisation within both spaces.

The historical roots of such state–civil society relationships can be traced to struggles over state power during and following British colonial rule. The victorious coalition pursued export-oriented industrialisation (EOI) led by international capital, alongside key roles in economic and social development for state capitalist enterprises and bureaucracies. A virtual class of technocratic politico-bureaucrats emerged, whose considerable powers and resources were, and remain, rationalised by elitist ideology asserting that Singapore's social and political order must reflect a 'meritocracy' (Tan 2012; Barr 2014a).

This ideology plays down the normative and political nature of conflict, emphasising instead apolitical problem-solving that technocratic elites are best placed to provide. Complementing this ideology is a moral notion of political accountability by ruling PAP leaders, equally hostile to civil society as a site through which powers and decisions of politico-bureaucrats can be contested. In this non-democratic republican variant of accountability ideology, the moral character and integrity of the elite are claimed as the primary checks against abuses of office and power – not liberal or democratic institutions (see Rodan and Hughes 2014: chapter 3).

Yet conflict emanating from, and/or compounded by, contradictions inherent to the PAP's development model has also meant that protecting existing state powers from effective scrutiny and contestation has faced challenges. Hence, innovations in state-sponsored MOPs giving special emphasis to non-democratic consultative and particularist ideologies of political participation; and continual refinements and additions to legislative curbs on civil society. The common strategic thread is the attempt to politically fragment reformist social forces so that independent collective mobilisation and action is limited or obstructed.

This strategy has been remarkably successful, but it has also ensured that underlying popular concerns – particularly related to structural inequality – have not been adequately addressed. Consequently, there has periodically been significant working-class support for opposition parties, the political impact of which has been contained by electoral gerrymandering and malapportionment (Tan and Grofman 2018; Ngiam 2020).

2.1 State–Civil Society Foundations

During the 1950s push for political independence from the British, independent trade union, student, cultural, and ethnic organisations were all active in civil society (Clutterbuck 1973: 100). The PAP formed in 1954 in an alliance between diverse but predominantly Chinese-language-educated popular forces on the one hand, and English-educated middle-class nationalists led by Lee Kuan Yew on the other. The former availed the PAP of mass organisational bases for electoral politics, the latter offered leftists cover of apparent political moderation (Josey 1974). Dominant fractions of the domestic bourgeoisie were so closely integrated with colonial capitalism that they displayed little interest in Singapore's self-government. Consequently, when that day came, they lacked political influence.

Following the PAP's resounding 1959 win in self-government elections, internal tensions led to a separate party – the *Barisan Sosialis* (Socialist Front, or *BS*) – formed by the leftists in 1961. The PAP responded by harassing opponents and critics, seeking to erode their social and political bases in civil society (Deyo 1981; Barr 2010). The PAP also amended the Societies Act in 1968, barring political engagement by organisations not specifically registered for such purpose.[7] In practice, this legislation exempted organisations expressing political support for, or aligning with, the PAP.

---

[7] See Tan (2017) on regulations covering public gatherings and the expression and dissemination of dissenting views.

Meanwhile, the PAP's structures were modified to institutionalise top-down executive control, including over recruitment and candidate selection, promoting ideological conformity and elite political cohesion (Barr 2014a; Tan 2020: 126–7). Independent labour organisations were also replaced with PAP-affiliated unions under the National Trades Union Congress (NTUC). State-controlled educational and cultural institutions to propagate PAP worldviews and accounts of Singapore's political history, as well as the monopoly of domestic media by government-linked companies (GLCs), were also integral to forging PAP political and ideological hegemony (Seow 1998; Rodan 2004; Barr 2019).

In short, state power was transformed to fundamentally reshape the permissible margins and forms of contestation open through both informal and formal political spaces of civil society.

Crucially, authoritarianism, globalisation, and a particular variant of state capitalism combined to consolidate and deepen the power of politico-bureaucratic elites. These elites ensured the social, physical, and technical conditions for cost-competitive industrial exports by international capital. State economic and social investments were also critical during the 1960s and 1970s in raising living standards that cultivated electoral support for the PAP (Rodan 1989; Tremewan 1994; Chua 1997). A vast range of GLCs subsequently proliferated, dominating the upper echelons of the domestic economy, leading to massive international investment portfolios and national reserves (Braunstein 2019: 90–7). The power and resources at the disposal of technocratic elites rose accordingly.

The same development model sowed seeds of future conflict. It simultaneously relies on large numbers of foreign workers or immigrants, respectively, at the least, and most, skilled ends of the economic spectrum. With no independent trade union advocacy, the working class would increasingly suffer the adverse market impact of low-wage foreign workers and industrial restructuring. Rising costs from the influx of well-remunerated foreign professionals and executives would also be felt by elements among the expanded and socially diversified middle class.

The PAP's ability to ensure that civil society expression does not become an avenue for seriously challenging the policies, interests, and ideologies of politico-bureaucratic elites would thus be tested.

2.2 Conflict Management and New MOPs

Political co-option was integral to the PAP's strategy of authoritarian rule established in the 1960s. Alongside the NTUC, an extensive range of para-political grassroots community organisations successfully articulated with the one-party state to mobilise PAP support (Seah 1973). However, a 12.9 per cent swing to opposition parties at the 1984 general election precipitated new political institution building by the PAP meant to contain conflicts linked to pressures and social changes associated with capitalist development.

The stunning boost in opposition support occurred in a context of social disruption linked to industrial restructuring driven by rising global cost competition in EOI (Rodan 1989: 142–88). Lee Kuan Yew's 1983 enunciation on eugenics – and accompanying social engineering plans – had also engendered disquiet among many of Singapore's increasing number of educated women. Lee worried that graduate women producing less offspring would dilute Singapore's talent pool. This reflected Lee's long-held elitist belief that Singapore's fate relied on 'no more than 5 per cent' who were 'more than ordinarily endowed physically and mentally' (in Chan 1985: 707). The PAP post-mortem on the 1984 election observed a rapidly expanding younger middle-class constituency, of which these women were one element (Chua 1994: 659).

Working-class opposition support was the principal dynamic in 1984, and in PAP vote share falls at the 1988 and 1991 elections. All opposition seats secured were in predominantly working-class constituencies. However, PAP leaders did not want Singapore's new middle class evolving into a conduit for anything approximating the revival of civil society expression akin to that snuffed out in the 1960s. Rising expectations among the well educated of a greater say in public policy was entirely consistent with the elitist meritocracy ideology of the PAP. The PAP sought to manage this contradiction.

Several small NGOs led by professionals, academics, and other middle-class elements advocating for policy reforms did emerge or reactivate during the mid-1980s and early 1990s. This included groups advocating for feminist, environmental, conservation, and racial equality issues. Subsequently, the number and the range of issues expanded to include human rights, problems of migrant workers, animal welfare, concerns of artistic communities, and many other issues (Soon and Koh 2017: xvii–xxiii).

The PAP strategy was to shape rather than completely block civil society expression, including through new MOPs. The rationale for this direction by PAP leaders emphasised the importance of participation for consensus building, and the problem-solving utility of drawing on additional knowledge and information (see Goh 1986; Lee, H.L. 1999).

New MOPs of societal incorporation and/or administrative incorporation started in 1985 with public policy feedback mechanisms under the Feedback Unit (FU), revamped in 2006 and renamed Reaching Everyone for Active

Citizenship @ Home (REACH). Separate government-led committees of inquiry involving public participation also emerged, the first of which reported in 1986 and the most recent of which was the year-long Our Singapore Conversation (OSC) that reported in 2013. Constitutional reform in 1990 paved the way too for nominated members of parliament (NMPs). NMPs are publicly nominated to a PAP-dominated parliamentary select committee recommending on appointments. NMPs can vote on most bills and motions, but not those concerning public funds, constitutional amendments, or no confidence in the government.

These MOPs employed consultative and/or particularist ideologies of representation to rationalise who can participate, how, and on what in feedback and deliberations over public policy. The capacity and inclination of the PAP to introduce such MOPs reflected the interests and ideologies of Singapore's politico-bureaucratic elites, but their timing also linked to Singapore's dynamic political economy and the contradictions therein.

For example, in 2005, the government decided to substantially increase the intake of foreign workers to maximise economic growth opportunities (Barr 2014b). Foreign labour would account for one-third of Singapore's total workforce by 2010. Immigration policies to further support this model also contributed to 32 per cent of Singapore's population growth during 2000–2014 (Chun 2013b). In the process, the trend towards rising economic inequality gathered momentum. The Gini coefficient increased from 0.42 to 0.49 between 2000 and 2012 (Chun 2013a), while absolute poverty was estimated at 11–12 per cent in 2011 (Chun 2013b).

One result of these changes was electoral. At the 2006 polls, support for opposition parties increased by 2.7 per cent to 33.4 per cent, and was especially pronounced in working-class districts (*New York Times* 2006). Concerns about immigration and foreign worker levels, public health, public transport, employment, and income inequality were thematic. Significantly, there was an unprecedented use of the Internet for independent social and political commentary in the approach to the 2006 polls (Weiss 2014: 872). Against this background, FU was relaunched as REACH, resulting in a concerted attempt through Facebook, Twitter, and Instagram accounts to engage Singaporeans on such issues. However, the 2011 election delivered the PAP 60.1 per cent of the vote, its lowest vote share since independence in 1965, prompting the introduction of the OSC to supplement the activities of REACH.

Kenneth Tan (2012) went so far as to argue that contradictions in the prevailing state and global capital relationship, in this neoliberal phase, resulted in the ideological edifice attached to it beginning to generate hegemonic challenges.

Approaching the 2015 general election, the PAP linked OSC processes to policy announcements involving greater social redistribution indicative of the shift towards a 'compassionate meritocracy' (Lee 2013). New funding commitments to healthcare, public housing, education, and income supplements helped to deliver a 9.7 per cent electoral swing back to the PAP that secured eighty-three of the eighty-nine seats on offer. It appeared that the PAP's latest non-democratic MOP innovation had helped return Singapore's elections to 'normal'.

However, in the 2020 general election the opposition regained 8.7 per cent support to give it a 39 per cent share of the total vote. This translated into the highest number of opposition seats since independence – ten out of ninety-three. Many voters' policy concerns remained unresolved, particularly those structurally linked to the unequal distribution of costs and benefits under Singapore's capitalist development model.

Of all the new MOPs meant to contain conflict, NMPs have a special significance. As with other new MOPs, NMP appointments have drawn in a range of pro-PAP forces and other actors from professional and voluntary communities. Yet here actors from select non-PAP-aligned CSOs and NGOs are also incorporated.

Official rationales for NMPs are couched in technocratic and diversity arguments: to inject 'independent and non-partisan views' into parliament and incorporate both talented people with expertise and underrepresented sections of society (Goh 1989; *STWOE* 1989).[8] As conflicts accompanying Singapore's development evolved, so too have group categories from which nominations are invited, promoting a multitude of seemingly self-contained policy areas militating against reformist coalitions.[9]

Nevertheless, the scheme has proved attractive for select reformist voices from Singapore's small group of informal civil society organisations. This includes leaders and members of NGOs such as the Nature Society of Singapore (NSS), the Association of Women for Action and Research (AWARE), the Association of Muslim Professionals (AMP), and Transient Workers Count Too (TWC2). Other individuals with progressive reformist agendas, notably concerning the arts sector, have also been appointed. Many of these activists participate to pursue issues they consider either neglected or underexplored by political parties – including opposition parties (Rodan 2018: 88).

Technically, upon entering parliament, appointed activists depart from *collective* civil society expression in favour of *individual* expression. They are perceived by elected opposition party representatives as antithetical to

---

[8] NMPs are appointed by the President on the advice of a parliamentary Special Select Committee.
[9] For fuller analysis of constraints on reformist coalition formation through NMPs, see Rodan (2018: chapter 4).

parliamentary democracy. The scheme has introduced more diversity to issues raised in parliament and provided a platform for a small number of activists to occasionally challenge core PAP policies and ideologies. However, the sole significant legislative impact of NMPs is the 1994 Maintenance of Parents Bill – mirroring PAP views on filial piety. How, then, has collective activism fared outside new MOPs?

2.3 Limits to Autonomous Space

A government-led *Singapore 21* report in 1999 identified 'active citizenship' as a 'core ideal in Singapore's future'. Leaders also warned citizens against political participation ignoring 'OB' (out of bounds) markers – a vague reference to activities outside formal politics (Lee 2005: 143–4). What constitutes 'politics' – as opposed to 'active citizenship' – is left to activists to test in practice. Those to have done this have tread carefully.

According to Soon and Koh (2017: xxviii), the growth and range of civil society groups emerging in Singapore in the past two decades is indicative of a post-materialist society, 'where basic physical, economic and material needs for many have been satisfied and remain important, but are superseded by the values of individual expression, autonomy, care of the other, the environment and animals'. However, the complexion of civil society is shaped by state power. The PAP's notion of active citizenship does not tolerate, for example, a revival of well-organised independent trade unions to better represent the concerns of many not faring so well materially.

Brief examination of different reform strategies for migrant labour and LGBT rights[10] illustrates the possibilities and constraints posed by state power structures for civil society expression. Attempts to conceal, rather than highlight, political or ideological differences with the PAP are thematic to both strategies.

Barred from joining or forming a trade union, migrant workers are steered down a path of administrative incorporation: required to channel individual grievances through complaints mechanisms within the Ministry of Manpower (MOM). However, Singapore's two dedicated advocates on behalf of migrant workers – TWC2 and Humanitarian Organisation for Migration Economics (HOME) – have sought to both engage with, and reform, the migrant labour regime.

Drawing on the MOP framework, Bal (2016) analysed participation by these NGOs across state-sponsored and autonomous sites of contestation. Registered as 'voluntary welfare organisations' (VWOs) under the Societies Act, HOME,

---

[10] LGBT is the acronym most used in Singapore; LGBTIQ+ is one of several alternatives.

and TWC2 are barred from political activity. However, VWO status allows them to undertake para-bureaucratic interventions into conciliation processes, activated when worker complaints are formally referred to the MOM by NGOs. In this way, administrative incorporation of the individual worker procedurally facilitates societal incorporation of NGOs.

Through correspondence with individual case officers and their departmental heads, as well as conciliation meetings, NGOs have found opportunities to request tighter adherence to labour laws (Bal 2016: 181–2). NGOs have also successfully lobbied through formal complaints channels for exceptional measures to protect workers' interests. Such was the case when unemployed Bangladeshi construction and shipyard workers affected by the 2008/2009 global financial crisis were allowed to seek new employers. Closed door meetings have also been used to lobby officials to modify the way existing laws and regulations are applied, or to advocate changes to them to their superiors (Bal 2016: 183).

Autonomous forms of political participation by HOME and TWC2 involve public lobbying of Ministers for labour reform via letters, statements, and commentaries to state-controlled and independent Internet media – including the dissemination of open letters to authorities. Public reporting of human and labour rights violations in conjunction with the reporting activities of the UN Council of Human Rights and the US State Department has also been adopted to raise awareness of worker indebtedness, illegal withholding of wages and passports (Bal 2016: 184).

Results from this dual strategy have been modest, with no systematic address of the migrant labour regime called for by HOME and TWC2. Moreover, according to Bal (2016: 197), reforms such as prohibiting employer kickbacks for worker recruitment and the establishment of a Migrant Workers Centre headed by a PAP MP 'encourage workplace disputes to be resolved administratively at an individual (individual worker or workers from an individual firm) level rather than through collective mobilisation'.

Meanwhile, the consequences for independent collective action by workers remain harsh. A spontaneous strike by 171 immigrant Chinese bus drivers with the state-owned mass rapid transit company SMRT Corp. in 2012 led to twenty-nine deportations and jail for five others. In a separate dispute that year at a Panasonic factory, a workers' petition to MOM for increased wages and reduced working hours was rejected. Following disquiet from MOM, the HOME executive director who assisted workers draw up the petition was redeployed and no longer directly engaged with MOM (Bal 2016: 198).

NGOs were more successful for a different category of foreign workers: those hired as domestic live-in nannies, cleaners, and cooks. After years of advocacy by HOME and TWC2, from January 2013, these workers were finally entitled to one day of rest per week. This decision occurred amidst a looming labour supply crisis for Singapore. These workers are pivotal to sustaining career options and lifestyles of Singapore's middle class (Koh et al. 2017: 196). The government also collects substantial revenue from levies on employers for domestic worker visas. Only when these interests were threatened did reform happen.

Similarly, sustained lobbying by HOME and TWC2 over working and social conditions in construction, manufacturing, and shipping sectors – particularly the cramped and poor sanitation standards of dormitories – was ignored by government (Han 2020c). GLCs are major foreign worker employers in both construction and shipping sectors. It took the advent of COVID-19 pandemic – when these conditions constituted a serious public health risk and a threat to the viability of core sectors of the economy (Lim 2020) – for some changes (Kathiravelu 2020).

Authorities' receptiveness to 'rational' and 'constructive' public policy suggestions is clearly filtered by calculations about the implications for the interests of the dominant bloc of social forces. LGBT rights activism has faced similar constraints.

LGBT activism can be traced to the formation in 1993 of People Like Us (PLU), whose applications in 1996 and 1997 for formal recognition were rejected. A permit application to hold a public forum on 'the role of gays and lesbians within Singapore 21' in 2000 was also refused, police explaining that 'it would be contrary to the public interest' as 'the Penal Code has provisions against certain homosexual practices' (in Peterson 2001: 134) – a reference to 377A of the Code. When the Societies Act was amended in 2004 to expedite applications, PLU again applied to register but with no more success.

Activists thus adopted what Lynette Chua (2014: x) characterises as a strategy of 'pragmatic resistance', whereby Singapore's gay activists nimbly adjust, escalate, or scale back their tactics as formal law and political norms change. Activists eschew law breaking, directly confronting the state, or being seen as a threat to existing formal power structures. This has included linking calls for greater equality with official emphasis on social harmony, as well as to the idea of retaining and attracting talent to benefit the economy (Chua 2014: 5).

The movement started building with its inaugural annual pride festival in 2005, expanding rapidly from 2009 with the first of what became annual Pink Dot rallies that grew from 2,500 attendees to 28,000 by 2015 (Soon and Koh 2017: xviii–xix). These initiatives capitalised on the government's introduction of a Speakers' Corner as a designated and regulated 'free speech area' for Singaporean residents, located at the inner-city Hong Lim Park. This obviated the need to apply for a license under the Public Entertainments Act for a public assembly. A further amendment in 2002 permitted exhibitions and performances at Speakers' Corner.

Pink Dot self-described as a 'congregation of people who believe that everyone deserves the right to love, regardless of their sexual orientation' (Jerusalem 2018). The movement also sought to have Section 377A repealed and submitted a parliamentary petition to that end in 2007, following the announcement of a comprehensive review of the Penal Code. Yet this reform aim was not mentioned at the Pink Dot rallies in the first six years. When NMP Siew Kum Hong presented the petition in parliament in 2007 to decriminalise homosexuality in the debate over the Penal Code (Amendment) Bill, neither the government nor opposition embraced the proposal (Rodan 2018: 85).

Importantly, the movement was not ignored outside parliament, social conservatives mobilising in reaction. This included Christian women securing nine of the twelve seats in 2009 on the AWARE executive committee, following a flurry of new memberships. That dominance was reversed the same year at an extraordinary meeting. Facebook was also harnessed against the LGBT movement, while various public and private institutions – including the National Library – came under pressure from Christian and Muslim organisations (Han 2020b). Civil society became the battleground between competing particularist identity ideologies of sexuality, gender, and religion.

This conflict contributed to the LGBT movement's political education. So too did opposition campaigns of the 2011 election, marked by increased challenges to PAP ideas and claims (Rodan 2016). Pink Dot began releasing statements and posting articles on social media (Han 2020b). By the 2019 rally, the message was more focussed, blunt, and directed solely at the government: 'REPEAL 377A'. The High Court subsequently dismissed three separate legal challenges to 377A (Taylor 2020).

'Pragmatic resistance' appeared no closer to realising this key reform goal. Yet the PAP government had not been entirely dismissive of arguments that the law poses a threat to the attraction of talent essential to the economy. The decision to no longer enforce – nor repeal – 377A was a concession to this argument, and one that Prime Minister Lee considered at the time adequate to safeguard talent attraction (Ng 2019). As with the rest day reform advocated by TWC2 and HOME, this concession was a reform issue intersecting at a certain political economy juncture with the interests of the dominant bloc.

Coalition building is necessary for the LGBT movement to cultivate greater support, but its prevailing conceptions of 'inclusivity' and 'diversity' are class constrained. As gay social and political activist Jolovan Wham observed: 'The language of resistance they [middle-class activists] have will be very different from the language of resistance that transgender sex workers have' (in Han 2020a). Linking the movement to broader, systemic struggles over inequality around 'social justice' would potentially connect middle-class and working-class elements. It might also falter over divisions within the movement between liberal and social democratic reform goals.

To varying degrees, racial, ethnic, religious, or some other particularist ideology militate against the formation of broader reformist coalitions in Singapore. So too does accommodation to – and in many cases the embrace of – the ideological notion that 'rational' and 'constructive' politics is preferable to explicit normative struggles over the use and control of state power.

As Ortmann (2015: 129–31) highlighted, limited attempts at oppositional coalitions in civil society have tended to stumble due to internal NGO tensions over appearing politically partisan in authorities' eyes. Yet he also detects 'coalitional capital' potential aided by the Internet (Ortmann 2015: 120). The campaign to prevent a proposed expressway that would decimate Singapore's historic Chinese cemetery in Bukit Brown was considered emblematic of such a trend.

Starting in late 2011 and for the best part of the rest of the decade, actors and organisations with ecological, cultural, and historical interests collaborated to contest and cooperate with government agencies to try and preserve the cemetery. The protracted campaign included online support networks such as the Facebook interest group 'All Things Bukit Brown' and a similarly named blog. The government proceeded with the expressway, but also committed to support various projects in recognition of Bukit Brown's natural, historical, and cultural significance (CAPE 2019).

Ortmann's point was not that this marked a civil society policy victory, but that it demonstrated a new degree of civil society cooperation. However, under the MOP framework, the most important indicator of the political significance of coalitions is not the number of interests or members encompassed, nor how long they sustain. Instead, it is the scale and nature of political conflict over state power they can engage in. On this criterion, PAP concerns about the potential political utility of electronic media for civil society lie elsewhere: with the activities of groups and individuals engaging in formal and informal political competition with the PAP's ideas – not those unthreatening to them.

2.4 Harnessing and Containing the Internet

Political fragmentation of Singapore's civil society not only reflects divergent interests and ideologies underpinning critiques of prevailing policies and state power relations, but also the impact of legislation targeting civil society and individual expressions. PAP leaders have adopted increasingly repressive measures to try and contain uses of the Internet and social media threatening their control over the limits to political and ideological contestation.

During the 2006 election battles, PAP opponents and critics combined explicitly political blogs with podcasting and vodcasting of campaign events to good effect. However, the 2011 election campaigns marked a quantum leap in the volume, range, and sophistication of integrating social media platforms with political mobilisation (Weiss 2014: 872). Shortly after, politically oriented news websites were targeted by the authorities through a new twenty-four-hour notice-and-take-down system which could result in fines and shutdowns for websites. A license system was also introduced barring websites from receiving loans and grants from foreign foundations.

The Protection from Online Falsehoods and Manipulation Act (POFMA) came into effect too in October 2019. The official pretext for POFMA was to combat alleged falsehoods that officials considered hurt the public interest, influence elections, incite hatred between different groups, and affect confidence in the Government and its entities. POFMA does not specify how a statement is determined to be 'false' nor what constitutes 'public interest'. It affords powers to government ministers and state authorities to interpret and act on these concepts, including enforced amendments to 'correct' online posts through to disabling access to online information.

By the eve of the 10 July 2020 election, POFMA had been invoked fifty-five times. Approximately two-thirds of these cases involved independent online media and one-quarter involved opposition politicians or activists. Nearly 85 per cent of flagged posts concerned negative portrayals of government actions or policies in relation to debates on such topics as the mismanagement of public funds, corruption, and discrimination against Singaporean nationals in favour of foreigners (Meyer 2020).

POFMA was integral to the PAP's intimidatory tactics during the 2020 election campaign. Numerous correction orders were issued against opposition candidates (Geddie 2020). Other Acts were also utilised to target activists from formal and informal civil society organisations. Meanwhile, apparent violations of these Acts by pro-PAP forces were swiftly dismissed by authorities or not acted on (Rodan 2020; *Online Citizen* 2021).

2.5 PAP Hegemony: Not Done with Yet

Despite ramped up new state-sponsored MOPs – and repression by the PAP – 39 per cent of Singaporeans supported opposition parties at the 2020 elections. Social and political contradictions inherent to Singapore's model of capitalist development generated and intensified conflicts not sufficiently neutralised or addressed through such MOPs. Thus, working-class Singaporeans feeling left behind in the 'Singapore economic miracle' looked more to the ballot than these MOPs. Elements of Singapore's middle class are also increasingly questioning the acute concentration of state power in the hands of the techno-cratic politico-bureaucratic elites.

However, the extent to, and depth of, rejection of core PAP ideologies is unclear. In the last two elections, there have been spectacular shifts in support to and from the PAP. The social democratic Workers' Party (WP), that holds all ten opposition seats in the fourteenth parliament (2020 –), has also avoided appearing ideological, keeping the focus tightly on specific policy differences with the PAP. Few among the ten opposition parties that contested the 2020 election are explicitly ideological, let alone offering a coherent ideological counter to the PAP worldview.

Singapore's model of capitalist development affords considerable powers to technocratic politico-bureaucrats under authoritarian rule. These powers are justified on the ideological grounds that rule by meritocratic elites of integrity is the necessary condition for economic and social development. Politics must be put aside in favour of rational problem-solving. This can benefit from consult-ation, but not be confused with claims to social citizenship rights or political conflict. A counter-hegemonic movement would necessarily have to reject and replace these interrelated propositions.

Towards pre-empting such a movement, the PAP's strategy is likely to remain founded on keeping critics and opponents in civil society politically fragmented and operating within limited margins of contestation.

3 Crony Capitalism, Race, and Civil Society Coalitions in Malaysia

Malaysia's contemporary political economy dynamics are fundamentally shaped by a racialised political project of state capitalism. This project has involved state cultivation and consolidation of a Malay bourgeoisie and related powers of a Malay politico-bureaucratic elite. Both were deemed essential by Malay nationalists following racial riots in 1969, amidst concerns of a widening socio-economic gap between ethnic Malays and others. However, affirmative action to address such concerns raised the stakes among factions competing for patronage within UMNO – the dominant party in ruling coalitions for the first six decades following Malaysia's political independence in 1957.

Capitalist development in Malaysia has thus been accompanied by periodic intra-party conflict over the spoils of state patronage, while popular disquiet over corruption, social and material inequality, and abuses of state power has been a catalyst for the emergence of civil society coalitions and mass mobilisations, variously seeking to defend or transform state power relations. Particularist ideologies of race, ethnicity, and religion have been especially influential in mediating these complex struggles, either contending or articulating with liberal and social democratic ideologies.

Malaysia's political regime is rationalised therefore not by claims of 'meritocracy', as in Singapore, but by the need for ethnic Malay political supremacy. Brief experiments with new MOPs involving societal incorporation and consultative ideologies to contain conflict in Malaysia failed, providing unintended platforms for critical scrutiny of state governance practices, public policies, and related ideological rationales of race, ethnicity, and religion. They also delivered no reforms. Malaysian activists have thus looked to civil society expression on a scale – and in ways – different from in Singapore, including coalitions within and between independent social organisations and political parties.

Social forces operating through civil society expression in Malaysia have included an extensive range of grassroots organisations of racial, religious, and/ or ethnic identities, many of which are formally aligned with *BN* political parties. They also include NGOs not formally aligned with *BN* parties but that prosecute similar ideologies, often to criticise and pressure *BN* parties. These organisations span rural and urban communities and incorporate diverse social classes. NGOs promoting variants of democratic ideologies are less extensive, generally led by middle-class professionals, based in urban centres. They are often small and focussed on specific issues, including social justice, human rights, environmentalism, governance, and gender equality. Significant alignments between these NGOs and opposition political parties can and have occurred, as have even broader coalitions across ideological lines at junctures of heightened conflict linked to Malaysia's political economy dynamics.

During the 1997–1998 Asian financial crisis (AFC), for example, differences among government leaders over which patronage networks and crony capitalists should be protected or exposed precipitated a multi-ethnic *reformasi* movement that – while unsuccessful in demands for a diverse raft of social, economic, political, and governance changes – substantially elevated the role of civil society expression in both its party-political and informal political spaces and indeed articulations between them (see Hilley 2001: 209–23).

Subsequently, social and material inequalities intensified under neoliberal policies – not least among ethnic Malays – contradicting official ideology equating the profitability of private Malay entrepreneurs and UMNO's political supremacy with the general uplifting of Malays. Civil society mobilisations increased accordingly, escalating following corruption allegations against

Prime Minister Najib in 2015 over US\$4.5 billion missing from state invest-ment company 1Malaysia Development Berhad (1MDB). Indeed, civil society coalitions were crucial to the electoral defeat of the *BN*, in the first change of government since independence in 2018.

Yet the *PH* collapsed within two years when the ethnic Malay *Parti Pribumi Bersatu Malaysia* (*PPBM, Bersatu,* or Malaysia United Indigenous Party) withdrew and formed the minority *Perikatan Nasional* (National Alliance, or *PN*) coalition government, with support from UMNO and other mainly ethnic Malay parties. The rise and fall of the *PH* government – and its aftermath – reflect a dynamic struggle over state power within which particularist ideologies of ethnicity, race, and religion remain pervasive, even if increasingly contested.

3.1 State–Civil Society Foundations

The roots of Malaysia's contemporary ethnic particularism were planted during colonial capitalism, under which policies were used to allocate ethnic Malays as well as immigrant ethnic Chinese and Indian communities to distinct capital and labour market roles (Puthucheary 1960). Therefore, structural inequalities could readily be interpreted through ethnic ideological and political lenses. This was reinforced by the way that authorities engaged with and promoted ethnic elites and their organisations leading to the Federation of Malaysia in 1948 and Malayan independence in 1957. In the process, Malay aristocratic forces effect-ively hijacked the nationalist movement at the expense of a more pan-Malayan vision (Amoroso 2014). Ethnic Malays and indigenous people of Sarawak and Sabah – collectively referred to as *Bumiputeras* ('sons of soil') and accounting for around half the population – were thus bestowed 'special positions' under the 1957 Constitution.

Class-based ideas of solidarity and organisations through which peasant and worker interests could be represented were discouraged (Nonini 2015: 36–9). In 1948, the Malayan Communist Party and the Pan-Malayan Federation of Trade Unions were banned, and most left-wing organisations were also banned within a few years (Mohammad 2009: 121). Over the next two decades, the communist bogey was the rationale for further repression (see Munro-Kua 1996: 40–57). With the deregistration of the Labour Party in 1972, the basis for any significant class-based or cross-class alternatives to ethnic politics was extinguished.

However, the framework of ethnic representation and inter-ethnic power sharing under the Alliance coalition ruling from 1957 until 1969 – comprising UMNO, the Malayan Chinese Association (MCA) and the Malayan Indian Congress (MIC) – failed to satisfy the expectations of impoverished ethnic Malays or deliver social harmony. Thus, in May 1969 general elections, the

Alliance secured just 48.5 per cent of the popular vote in peninsula Malaysia while opposition ethnic Chinese parties made big gains. Polls were suspended for other states (Wong and Othman 2009: 12), followed by race riots.

Elites responded by boosting the ideological and institutional role of ethnicity. Central to this was the New Economic Policy (NEP) announced in 1970 emphasising state promotion of an ethnic Malay bourgeoisie and a range of distributional policies targeting ethnic Malays in general (Gomez and Saravanamutta 2013). State patronage was mediated by considerations of how to strengthen political bases for UMNO powerholders, including roles for regional 'warlords' and mid-level brokers (see Weiss 2020: 140). Under the *BN* ruling coalition formed in 1973, this system bred corruption and fuelled periodic patronage struggles between contending coalitions of party-political, bureaucratic, and business interests (Searle 1999; Gomez 2002). Such struggles often precipitated increased civil society and individual expression critical of ruling elites and their governance institutions.

This is precisely what happened during the 1980s following reforms to accelerate Malaysia's industrial transformation, resulting in over a hundred critics detained from October 1987 under the Internal Security Act's (ISA) *Operasi Lalang* (Weeding Operation) (Weiss 2006). Intra-elite friction and civil society activism also flared up in the 1990s, in an even more intense struggle over state power. Under the New Development Plan of 1990, Prime Minister Mahathir promoted new conglomerates through wide-ranging privatisations of state assets, with select business tycoons awarded privileged monopolies or oligopolies (Khoo 2006: 184). With the advent of the AFC, loans of many of these conglomerates were overexposed, something Mahathir intended to address through a government bailout and which his deputy Anwar Ibrahim opposed.

In UMNO's ensuing power struggle, Anwar was sacked and imprisoned on spurious sodomy charges that precipitated the formation of a breakaway *Parti Keadilan Nasional* (National Justice Party) and the unleashing of a *reformasi* movement encompassing new levels of cooperation between opposition parties and other activists in civil society. This movement comprised a variety of social forces collectively disgusted with corruption and other state power abuses, but its solutions ranged from democratic reform to the adoption of liberal good governance systems and stronger moral adherence to Islamic religious beliefs (Rodan and Hughes 2014: 60–2).

Reformasi produced huge demonstrations throughout 1999 and some opposition electoral gains, but momentum could not be sustained. Instead, ethnic and religious sensitivities generated increasing tensions and a return to sharper ideological divisions within civil society. But what were the implications of this for the preferred MOPs through which competing interests sought to progress or contain conflict?

3.2 Conflict Management and New MOPs

Attempts by *BN* to contain conflict through societal incorporation and consensus ideologies included two National Economic Consultative Councils (NECCs) – during 1989–1990 (NECC I) and 1999–2000 (NECC II) – to advise cabinet on major development plans.

NECC I was established amidst anxieties over the transition from the NEP to the New Development Plan. It incorporated 150 people including both democratically authorised representatives from political parties as well as appointments depicted as either representing specific interests or as injecting valuable apolitical expertise for good policy advice (Heng 1997). UMNO leaders were not ideologically committed to technocratic representation, but they saw tactical value in its potential to limit challenges to particularism.

Apart from two representatives from the Malaysian Trades Union Congress (MTUC), civil society representation of non-*BN* aligned organisations was mainly through individuals of assorted progressive causes, including consumer affairs, social justice, and women's rights advocacy. Enough diversity of interests and perspectives was incorporated that custodians of the prevailing affirmative action policies had to grapple with liberal arguments about market efficiency and meritocracy, and pressures for a needs-based approach to poverty eradication.

Indeed, recommendations in NECC I's interim report included the elimination of rentier elements, power abuse, corruption, discrimination, and waste in the implementation of the New Development Plan (Jomo 1994: 38). The report also called for enhanced public access to official data and the establishment of an independent monitor agency to oversee the plan's implementation.

However, such proposals precipitated a counter-reaction, with Prime Minister Mahathir declaring that the government was not bound by the recommendations. Several NECC members resigned, denouncing the exercise as farcical (Jomo 1994: 49; Mauzy 1995: 85). The final report prescribed qualified pro-market reforms geared towards managing intra-elite conflict and fostering mutual interests among different fractions of capital (see Heng 1997: 289).

NECC I disappointed reformists and alerted the *BN* to the risks of consultative institutions for *BN*'s political and ideological control. A decade later, though, political polarisation over *BN* responses to the AFC led to the launch of NECC II. Harsh police measures to quell *reformasi* movement street demonstrations and civil disobedience had failed and calls for Mahathir to resign to protect business interests mounted. In response, Mahathir linked NECC II to the need for a new strategy to address the interrelated challenges of economic globalisation and liberalisation (Lee, L.T. 1999).

Key political parties and NGO actors boycotted NECC II (Tay 1999). The government also failed in its attempts to incorporate representatives from an important and controversial component of the *reformasi* movement – the Malaysian Chinese Organisations' Election Appeals Committee, *Suqiu. Suqiu* involved eleven associations and its seventeen-point appeal was endorsed by more than two thousand other organisations (Weiss 2006: 135). NECC II attracted little media attention and its eventual report was not even made publicly available.

Consultative ideologies and institutions were discredited in reformists' eyes, confirming for them the importance of more independent civil society space – inside and outside parliament.

3.3 Civil Society Coalitions and *BN's* Defeat

Despite the impressive scale and range of forces mobilised through civil society during *reformasi, BN* leaders skilfully exploited issues of race and religion to resoundingly defeat the opposition *Barisan Alternatif* (Alternative Front) elect-oral coalition in 1999 and 2004 federal polls (Weiss 2006: 127–61). However, contradictions between official ideologies and outcomes of Malaysian capitalist development would intensify, enough to precipitate new coalitions in civil society ultimately contributing to *BN's* unseating in 2018. Cooperation was achieved, though, by downplaying ideological differences.

So devastating were the 2004 election results for the three major opposition parties – the multi-ethnic *Parti Keadilan Rakyat* (People's Justice Party, or *PKR*[11]), the ethnic-Malay *Parti Islam Se-Malaysia* (Pan-Malaysian Islamic Party, or *PAS*) and the predominantly ethnic Chinese Democratic Action Party (DAP) – that by 2005 they sought a new political strategy for challenging the *BN*. The result was the Joint Action Committee for Electoral Reform and the launch of *Gabungan Philihanraya Bersih dan Adil* (Coalition for Clean and Fair Elections, or *Bersih*) established in November 2006. Obstacles to free and fair elections were extensive, varied and systematically designed to favour the *BN* and particularly UMNO (Tsun 2010).

Bersih initially comprised five opposition political parties, the MTUC and twenty-four NGOs. These NGOs were predominantly small, single-issue organ-isations, several of which were centred on some aspect of human rights. Alongside the progressive multi-ethnic reform movement *Aliran*, there were

---

[11] *PKR* involved the merger in 2003 of *PKN* and the Malaysian People's Party.

also organisations whose principal activities or advocacies were ethnic in focus. By late 2014, sixty-two NGOs were involved, political parties had been dropped from its organisational membership, and *Bersih*'s campaign extended beyond its electoral institution reform demands while avoiding issues of social redistribution lest this reignite long-standing and unresolved ideological tensions among *BN* critics and opponents. Consequently, *Bersih*'s five mass mobilisations between 2007 and the 2018 election attracted Malaysians with widely varying political grievances and goals.

An unsatisfactory Electoral Commission (EC) response to *Bersih*'s initial reform demands led *PAS* activists to successfully argue that popular action was required to pressure authorities. Within *Bersih*, *PAS* had at its disposal the most nationally extensive – albeit religious-based – collective organisations for mass mobilisation. Demonstrations in Kuala Lumpur on 10 November 2007 attracted at least 40,000 supporters, police deploying tear gas and water cannons to disperse protesters, forty-six of whom were arrested (Lee 2008: 198).

Days out from the March 2008 general elections, the EC backed down on its earlier undertaking to *Bersih* that indelible ink would be used to identify electors who had already voted (Liew 2013: 302). This compounded concerns across ethnic groups about rising living costs, reduced government fuel subsidies, highway toll charges, job insecurity, and perceived increased crime in urban areas (Welsh 2013). The election result was unprecedented, with *BN* losing its two-thirds parliamentary majority and a pronounced leakage of non-Malay and urban votes. This bolstered the dominance of UMNO within the *BN*, fuelling more strident Islamic and ethnic Malay particularist ideologies and policies thereafter (Hamid and Razali 2015).

Social contradictions inherent to Malaysian capitalism gathered momentum in the years ahead. By 2012, for example, the wealth of Malaysia's forty richest people amounted to 22 per cent of the country's GDP, rising from 15.7 per cent in 2006 (UNDP 2014: 48–9). Meanwhile, selective neoliberal policies that benefited certain UMNO-linked conglomerates raised costs for others. This included increased privatisation of healthcare, hikes in private highway tolls, and rising rents affecting retailers in city centres. Public subsidies were reduced for electricity, tertiary education, petrol, and sugar, and a 6 per cent Goods and Services Tax was introduced (Rodan 2018: 201).

The 2008 elections resulted in *Pakatan Rakyat* (*PR*) parties forming government in the states of Penang and Selangor (as well as in Kelantan where *PAS* was returned) and a view within *PR* that national electoral reform advocacy should now be rationalised. Accordingly, in April 2010, *Bersih* was relaunched as *Bersih* 2.0 and non-party political civil society activists would lead mobilisations, although *PR* parties remained critical support bases. Behind this new division of labour lay differences among *PR* parties – and between MPs and NGO activists – over the desirability of reintroducing local elections (see Rodan 2018: 191–8).

Such divisions eventually generated tension within *Bersih*, but not before substantial mobilisations following the movement's disappointment with official responses under new Prime Minister Najib Razak. Indeed, authorities tried to prevent a March for Democracy in July 2011, including by declaring *Bersih* 2.0 an illegal organisation. Nevertheless, an estimated 50,000 protesters braved the streets, contending with tear gas, water cannons, and other police aggression (Khoo 2015). *PAS* grassroots organisations were again important to the scale and multi-ethnic complexion of demonstrators. There was also a rise in urban – especially Malay – youth participation in apparently spontaneous action, including through social media (Ong 2011).

So concerned was Najib that he established a Parliamentary Select Committee to recommend on electoral reforms. However, the resulting report was deemed inadequate by *Bersih* 2.0 leaders, triggering a third rally in April 2012 backed by eighty-four NGOs which authorities allowed to proceed. Around 100,000 protesters took to the streets (Gooch 2012). *Bersih* 2.0 had evolved into a powerful movement, but it encompassed a complex and contradictory array of elements. According to one *Bersih* organiser, possibly less than 10 per cent of protesters might have been committed to electoral reform (Rodan 2018: 201).

The subsequent May 2013 general election witnessed a recovery in the UMNO vote, but the *BN*'s vote share plummeted to just 47 per cent. The government was only returned due to acute electoral malapportionment.

Alongside *Bersih*'s apparent progress, election results also heightened tensions within *PAS* and between *PAS* and the DAP. The DAP now overtook *PKR* to command most parliamentary seats within the *PR* coalition. Meanwhile, *PAS* suffered losses to UMNO, which adopted more intense communalistic rhetoric in the lead up to the polls. Conservatives within *PAS* thus embarked on a reassertion of traditional Islamic values as a strategy to regain ground.

Containing tensions within *PR* was rendered even more difficult when its leader Anwar was again jailed in February 2015. It was a declaration by *PAS* conservatives – now in control of that party – to enact the Islamic code of hudud in the state of Kelantan that ultimately brought *PR*'s collapse. This was replaced by *PH*, comprising the *PKR*, DAP, and *Parti Amanah Negara* (*Amanah/PAN*, or National Trust Party) created by progressives who departed *PAS*.

The absence of a cohesive non-racial socially redistributive reform agenda among forces in civil society – either inside or outside parliament – meant that particularist ideologies of race and ethnicity and related conceptions of redistribution continued to prove seductive for many disadvantaged Malays. However, Prime Minister Najib and his government would soon be embroiled in the scandal over 1MDB, a wholly government-owned company of the Ministry of Finance established by Najib in 2009 purportedly to promote long-term economic opportunities via foreign investment and global partnerships. Najib also chaired 1MDB's advisory board. The scandal amplified and crystallised assorted sentiments of injustice over existing elite rule.

Bersih 2.0 capitalised on this, with its leader, Maria Chin Abdullah (in Kow 2015) announcing that a fourth rally would 'demand real democratisation to end corruption and save the economy'. This tactical pitch offered diverse concerns an avenue for protest.

Bersih leaders again defied authorities, this time with countrywide rallying, and during 29–30 August 2015 attracted crowds exceeding 100,000 in Kuala Lumpur alone (Blakkarly 2015). However, *PAS*'s refusal to mobilise supporters dented the Malay turnout. This prompted extreme elements of UMNO and other defenders in civil society of the existing political and economic regime to amplify their ideological and political attacks on *Bersih* 2.0. At a September 16 rally in 2015 of 'Red Shirts' organised by martial arts group Malaysian National Silat Federation, speakers portrayed *Bersih* 2.0 as an unacceptable challenge to Malay political supremacy and religious beliefs (Teoh 2015).

As UMNO's ideology became more contested, Najib increasingly courted other right-wing ethno-nationalist groups in civil society. *Pertubuhan Kebajikan dan Dakwah Islamiyah SeMalaysia* (*Pekida*, or Association of Islamic Welfare and Dakwah of Malaysia) and its vast network was among the most controversial. *Pekida* engaged in 'connivance militancy' involving subcontracted legal and/or illegal political actions, ranging from advocacy to demonstrations and violence (Lemiére 2014: 92–3).

Ironically, contradictions between democratic and non-democratic forces and ideologies within both *Bersih* 2.0 and opposition parties seeking Najib's resignation enabled former Prime Minister Mahathir (1981–2003) to insert himself at the pivot of this struggle. In office, Mahathir suppressed the *reformasi* movement and embedded political discrimination to undermine the independence and integrity of most of the institutions *Bersih* 2.0's reform demands targeted (Slater 2015). He and former deputy UMNO leader Muhyiddin teamed up with *Bersih* 2.0 in its fifth rally in Kuala Lumpur on 19 November 2016 to pressure Najib to resign.

By the 2018 elections, *Bersatu* – the newly established party of Mahathir, Muhyiddin, and other disillusioned UMNO exiles – was not only a member of the *PH* coalition, but Mahathir was its leader. It was thought that, with such an historic champion of UMNO as Mahathir at the helm, ethnic Malays could be reassured that it was 'safe' to cast their ballots with *PH,* blunting the assertions made by the regime leaders and groups like *Pekida*. In the event of a *PH* victory, though – and upon Anwar's release from prison – Mahathir agreed to hand over the prime ministerial reins to the rhetorical champion of a multi-ethnic Malaysia.

This strategy appeared to be vindicated on the election day of 9 May when – despite extensive repressive measures before and during the election campaigns to thwart *BN* opponents – *PH* secured a coalition government with 121 of the 222 seats contested. The platform that *PH* took to the elections embodied many of *Bersih* 2.0's reform plans to reshape the exercise of state power.

3.4 Transforming versus Consolidating State Power

Shortly after taking office, some *PH* leaders encapsulated the coalition's reform agenda as one driven by a vision of a 'New Malaysia', implying a decisive shift from race-based politics and policymaking. This rhetoric inspired both optimism and anxiety among different elements of the new government. It was also emphatically contested by well-organised forces within civil society. Resistance soon surfaced within the government to several core *PR* institutional reform commitments. The scale and ideological tone to civil society mobilisation against a 'New Malaysia' also emboldened forces within *PH* who positioned themselves as champions and defenders of Malay political supremacy (Afiq 2020).

Following the election, a concerted attempt was made by *Ikatan Muslimin Malaysia* (*ISMA*, or Malaysian Muslim Solidarity) leading a coalition of NGOs to counter the influence of the *Amanah*-aligned *Pertubuhan Ikram Malaysia* (*IKRAM*) among middle-class Muslims (Hew 2020). This included a rally on 28 July 2018 whose theme translated to 'Post-GE14 New Malaysia: Malay Muslims are being threatened'. The principal protest was over the government's proposed recognition of the United Examination Certificate (UEC), a standardised test adopted by independent ethnic Chinese high schools in Malaysia (Hew 2020). Demands were made to ensure no questioning of the special rights of Malays (see Perimbanayagam 2018).

The Malay insecurity theme was increasingly exploited in civil society mobilisations and related activities, especially following Prime Minister Mahathir's announcement in late September 2018 at the United Nations General Assembly that his government was looking to ratify all remaining international conventions. This included the International Convention on the

Elimination of All Forms of Racial Discrimination (ICERD). In response, an 8 December 2018 rally to protest organised by Muslim NGOs – backed by *PAS* and UMNO – attracted 60,000 people (Hew 2020).

By mid-November 2018, Mahathir had announced that the government would not proceed with ICRED's ratification. A similar announcement followed in April 2019 about another UN convention: the Rome Statute of the International Criminal Court (ICC). This was abandoned after protestations from members of Malaysia's royal family, including spurious claims that the Statute contradicted the Federal Constitution, would undermine royal institutions, and threaten 'the special status of the Malays as well as the sanctity of Islam in the country' (*The Star* 2019).

NGO activism asserting particularist ideologies of race and religion gathered further momentum in 2019, as did the courting of these sentiments by Mahathir and other members of *Bersatu*. Indeed, the demands became more strident and social forces seeking to defend existing state powers from proposed reforms more cohesive. In early October that year, four public universities – including the country's most prestigious, the University of Malaya (UM) – co-organised a Malay Dignity Congress attended by 5,000 people. This brought together elements from the dominant bloc of interests associated with Malaysia's established economic, political, and social institutions crafted under *BN* rule, including leaders of all Malay-majority political parties and a broad range of Islamic NGOs and influential muftis (Chin 2019).

The Congress' theme was blunt: the ideology of *Ketuanan Melayu* (Malay Supremacy) was beyond the permissible limits of political contestation. In his speech, the UM vice chancellor warned non-Malays that to go down this path would violate the social contract upon which the political order was premised. The Congress demanded that major government posts be exclusively reserved for Malays. Despite Malays already holding key portfolios and numerically dominating *PH* (Hassan 2018), in Mahathir's keynote speech he pronounced that his government was not Malay enough (Hassan 2019).

Alongside these ideological campaigns in civil society, Mahathir tried to insulate core institutions from reforms. In particular, he and his *Bersatu* colleagues sought to consolidate political control over GLCs and block or dilute measures for greater transparency and accountability in the governance of public institutions.

Mahathir established a Ministry of Economic Affairs (MEA), led by *Bersatu* Vice President Azmin Ali, which subsequently took control of some GLCs from the Ministry of Finance. Malaysia's sovereign wealth fund, *Khazanah Nasional*, was also transferred to the Prime Minister's Office. Azmin and Mahathir took up appointments to *Khazanah*'s board of directors, violating an explicit undertaking in *PH*'s election manifesto to bar politicians from such roles (Gomez 2019). Subsequently, MEA convened a Congress of the Future of Bumiputeras and the Nation, followed by the *Mid-term Review of the 11th Malaysia Plan* that re-committed to the key role of race-based discrimination through political patronage – not just for private business development, but to harness such support to electoral support strategies.

In view of these and other deviations from the *PH* platform, reformist NGOs and think tanks were also actively seeking to pressure policymakers. This included the formation in January 2019 of a GLC Reform Cluster to lobby for increased accountability and transparency among Malaysia's GLCs. Appointments to GLCs were especially contentious (Augustin 2019).

Some within *PH* attempted to explain the tardy implementation of moves towards a 'New Malaysia' as a function of obstacles from a 'deep state' (*Malaysiakini* 2019). However, much of the resistance came from within the *PH* – which was itself beset with competing preferences for who should exercise state power, how, and to what end. These ideological struggles reflected and incorporated competing forces in civil society.

Reformists were seeking a transformation of prevailing particularist ideologies of race and religion, but their redistributive programmes to transcend such ideologies were under-developed. This problem was partly ideological. Many reformists were most comfortable emphasising apolitical institutions to ensure merit prevailed over political patronage. It was also historical and structural. The comprehensive dismantling of class-based organisations militated against adequate bases in civil society through which alternatives to race-based redistribution could be conceived and promoted.

Such constraints made it easier for opponents of institutional and governance reforms to misrepresent and mobilise against such initiatives. This included within *PH* from members of *Bersatu*, who were ideologically clear sighted in seeking to conserve political patronage and money politics as a means not just for advancing their direct power ambitions (Welsh 2018: 375), but also as a *modus operandi* for race-based redistribution as the 'natural' solution to inequality. The struggle for control over state power was also shaped by competing political ambitions among ethnic Malay *PH* leaders with similar particularist ideological affinities – some of which began even before the 2018 elections (see Kassim 2020). It transpired that Mahathir was not prepared to relinquish the helm for Anwar, source enough to escalate intra-*PH* friction.

The government's collapse was ultimately instigated by *Bersatu*'s president, Muhyiddin, and deputy president, Azmin Ali, and supporters forming a new coalition with UMNO, *PAS* and other opposition parties. Malaysia's constitutional monarch, King Abdullah, determined in late February 2020 that the numbers were with Muhyiddin and allies, who thus formed the *PN* government without election. On 11 January 2021, in the context of the COVID-19 health crisis, the king and prime minister declared a state of emergency to be enforced until 1 August 2021. Laws on public assemblies, sedition, media were quickly exercised by the *PN* government to intimidate reformist forces in civil society.

However, the old political formula whereby UMNO exerted ideological and political control through formal political and state institutional power did not neatly resume. Instead, a dynamic reconfiguration of party politics and civil society alignments began, reflecting tensions among forces seeking to consolidate, enhance, or challenge positions within the dominant bloc of interests defining the political regime. Muhyiddin's replacement as prime minister by UMNO Vice President Ismail Sabri Yaakob in August 2021due to infighting within his ruling coalition was symptomatic of this tension.

3.5 Same Old? Not Quite

The societal incorporation MOP proved not to be a good political fit for the regime in Malaysia. Through it, particularist ideologies rationalising existing policies and state power structures serving the dominant bloc of interests came under critical scrutiny, but without any prospects of reform. Neither established elites nor their opponents found this MOP useful. Consequently, for both those seeking to defend or transform state power, formal and informal political spaces of civil society became even more important. As illustrated above, these contests have been dynamic and complex, periodically resulting in political coalitions containing both democratic and non-democratic ideologies.

The latest collapse of such a coalitional challenge to the political status quo – formally represented through *PH* – neither marks nor portends, the decline of activism through civil society in Malaysia. Civil society divisions are as significant among forces subscribing to particularist ideologies as they are with those seeking to transcend them. As Khoo (2020: 3) observed, 'the established projects of the Malay political class have run their course but an alternative project to replace it was aborted'. Multiple political parties now lay claim to protecting Malay rights, 'a sure sign that none of them has an uncontested claim' (Khoo 2020: 4).

It is impossible to explain these dynamic conflicts without understanding the social foundations underpinning them, namely 'a peculiar development of political economy that transformed UMNO's original raison d'être of Malay nationalism into a corporate imperative of Malay capitalism' (Khoo 2020: 10).

Contention over control and distribution of resources under this model of capitalism remain pivotal to the opportunities, constraints, and directions of efforts through civil society to shape state power in Malaysia.

4 Private Oligarchy, Civil Society, and Populism in the Philippines

State power relationships in the Philippines differ from those underpinning either Singapore's technocratic state capitalism or Malaysia's racialised form of state capitalism. In the Philippines, state power has been shaped from the outset by extreme concentrations of *private* wealth, power, and coercion – initially involving an agricultural landowning class – that consolidated through capitalist development and electoral democracy. Indeed, private economic and formal political power has been so closely intertwined in the Philippines that the concept of oligarchic capitalism best characterises the core dynamic of the country's political economy.

Conflict over inequality and governance are thematic to all three countries, but the capital accumulation strategies involved and the constellation of winners and losers from them necessarily differ. Networks of state corruption and political patronage in the Philippines, for instance, have continually facilitated profitable private capital accumulation strategies without generating adequate employment and income levels. Poverty has been an endemic problem.

Consequently, despite the Philippines boasting the region's most extensive volume and range of CSOs and assorted movements – as well as the longest history of electoral institutions[12] – it has also offered fertile ground for populist ideologies and leaders exploiting social divisions and conflicts inextricably linked to the political hegemony of oligarchic capitalism.

Groups in civil society include revolutionary peasant and working-class-based people's organisations (POs), only selectively engaged in electoral polit-ics; left-leaning social democrats operating through CSOs and political party politics; liberal democrats operating through party politics and small middle-class-led NGOs advocating on governance and social justice causes. Forces operating in and across formal and informal political spaces of civil society subscribe to competing ideologies of democracy in their respective attempts to transcend, reform, or contain oligarchic capitalism.

Shared interests between dominant capitalists and political elites have been so deep and systematic that forces in civil society have been routinely thwarted in attempts to reform state power. Periodic episodes of intra-elite friction have thus presented greatest opportunities for reformist civil society mobilisation, only to be followed by disappointment as oligarchic dominance is quickly

---

[12] The Philippines conducted its first general elections in 1907, during the colonial period.

reasserted. The most recent demonstration of this pattern is the 2016 rise to power of President Rodrigo Duterte and the ushering in of an authoritarian populism. Some reformist elements in civil society even held hopes that working with Duterte might result in structural change towards uplifting the poor, given Duterte's occasional socialist rhetoric.

Cross-class coalitions of support for Duterte reflect not just the limitations of liberal and other ideological challenges to oligarchic power – including through societal incorporation and consultative ideologies – prior to Duterte's presidency, but also the structural dynamics of oligarchic capitalism. One of Duterte's strongest support bases, for example, was ironically from Filipino overseas foreign workers (OFWs), who went abroad due to the chronic lack of employment opportunities, and those who benefited from repatriated funds of these OFWs.

Duterte's reshaping of state power proved unrelated to any reforms to the structural power of oligarchs. It was centred instead on enforcing a moral politics emphasising discipline and punishment of behavioural practices among the poor, of which his 'war on drugs' has been emblematic (Curato 2016). His authority to interpret morally correct behaviour was founded on his status as a charismatic and culturally authentic representative of 'the people'. This authenticity was framed not in collective values antithetical to the market, but in support of its individual and competitive nature. Projected cultural authenticity also provided the rationale for narrowing of civil society contestation over state power.

Before elaborating on these points, brief examination of the historical roots and dynamics of oligarchic capitalism that have both given cause for civil society reformism and helped keep it in check is in order.

4.1 State–Civil Society Foundations

The structures within which oligarchic capitalism in the Philippines operates are rooted in the mixed legacies of Spanish (1521–1898) and US (1899–1946) colonial rule: the former promoting centralised state apparatuses of power that facilitated the consolidation of oligarchic capitalism, the latter favouring more decentralisation (Wolters 1984: 14). The net effect was a distinctive pattern of state formation involving 'the emergence and entrenchment of small-town bosses, provincial "war-lords," and authoritarian presidents by providing mechanisms for private monopolisation of resources and prerogatives of the state' (Sidel 1999: 19).

Oligarchs have harnessed their political networks and private resources for various forms of primitive accumulation, and to secure state contracts, licenses, and favourable policies. They have also been utilised to shape the drawing of electoral boundaries to benefit oligarchs' interests, and to counter or intimidate threatening reformist voices in civil society through money politics or private armies. This is not a 'weak state', but one designed to enable the exercise of strong private power to consolidate and extend oligarchic interests.

The Philippines' economic modernisation began with the commercialisation of agriculture for export towards the end of the nineteenth century. This consolidated well into the next century under US colonial rule,[13] facilitated by preferential access to the US market. Meanwhile, in a classic colonial trade pattern, manufactures were imported from the United States and Europe. The transition to capitalist production relations through wage labour in agriculture was protracted and uneven, with varying forms of self-employment and exploit-ative semi-feudal land control arrangements persisting well into the future.

Where wage labour did expand significantly it was through large-scale agricultural processing factories, some of which were sites of periodic strike activity – especially in the 1930s amidst the establishment of the *Partido Komunista ng Pilipinas* (Communist Party of the Philippines, or CPP) and general cuts to wages in the Philippines (Hutchison 2006: 52). Labour-CPP links were short lived, though, the latter soon deemed an illegal organisation and its leaders jailed. In general, during American colonial rule, unions were, as Carroll (in Hutchison 2012: 42) observed, 'not specifically protected or encour-aged'. On the contrary, regulatory regimes and private intimidation compounded and reflected the disinterest among elected officials in issues of poverty and inequality (see Kunihara 1945; Wurfel 1959).[14]

Disdain for traditional politicians thus set in early, leading to widespread adoption by Filipinos of the pejorative term *trapos*. This referred to politicians, linked to a powerful capitalist, who bilked the state for their respective material gains (Abinales and Amoroso 2005: 240; Quimpo 2008: 4).

Popular disillusionment with electoral politics under oligarchic capitalism was dramatically illustrated in the peasant movement's unsuccessful armed Huk Rebellion (1946–1954) against the Philippine government to achieve land reform. As Kerkvliet (1977: 209) observed, the same concerns spread well beyond peasants, in a pervasive popular view that 'the government was in the hand of the elite, particularly the landlords, while the poor people had no influence in government and without influence there was no way to get justice'.

The economic bases of oligarchic capitalism would subsequently diversify in the 1950s into import substitution industrialisation under favourable

---

[13] The Philippines was colonised by the United States in 1898.

[14] Registered or otherwise, by 1940, just 5 per cent of the Philippines workforce was estimated to be organised (Hutchison 2006: 52).

government policies and American trade preferences. After initial promise, though, growth could not be sustained because income levels for the domestic population did not sufficiently rise (Hutchison 2006: 43). Ironically, this was a function of the successful constraints imposed on organised labour that oligarchs and their political allies had ensured. Thus, rent seeking opportunities in finance, real estate, and construction became more important. Although there were some tensions as new entrants emerged to challenge for the spoils of rent seeking, what united old and new oligarchs and allied politicians was a determination to block reform agendas threatening to their interrelated interests (de Dios and Hutchcroft 2003: 48).

4.2 Civil Society, People Power, and Class Conflict

It was not until the People Power overthrow of authoritarian rule under President Marcos in 1986 – referred to as EDSA[15] – that hopes of transcending oligarchic rule resurfaced. However, civil society forces were divided in their democratic visions and political strategies. Here we can broadly distinguish between revolutionary, radical, and moderate reformist forces and ideologies in civil society – divisions that remain relevant today.

Revolutionaries focus on building class-based and anti-(neo)imperialist organisations and mass mobilisations, to ultimately replace capitalism with socialism. Organising of peasants, workers, national minorities, and others through POs is the foundation for their National Democratic Front (NDF). Led by the CPP, this movement comprises thousands of organisations aligned with the *Bagong Alyansang Makabayan* (*Bayan*, New Patriotic Alliance, or NPA) (Törnquist 2013).

Moderate civil society activism emerged during the Cold War in reaction to communist influence among the poor, as Catholic Church-based CSOs took up assorted social justice causes. Following the fall of Marcos in 1986, moderates were well placed to shape civil society directions, especially through international aid programme funding. Yet, these opportunities favoured small cause-oriented NGOs at the expense of wider reform issues and movements (Lane 1990: 37–8). This direction was institutionalised in 1990 with the creation of the Caucus of Development Non-Governmental Organisations (CODE-NGO), operating as a base for the Liberal Party and comprising 1,600 affiliated organisations by 2013 (Porcalla 2013).

The EDSA middle-class-led coalition was not an intrinsically democratic force in civil society. It included oligarchs disgruntled with Marcos' centralised

---

[15] EDSA refers to the Metro Manila thoroughfare that was the site of major mobilisations against Marcos leading to the reinstatement of liberal democracy.

controls over resource patronage as well as liberal and conservative business and Catholic Church critics of Marcos. Nor could it be understood as comprised of 'good' and 'bad' elements. EDSA civil coalitions in civil instead embodied competing class interests that were to play out in continuing struggles over the extent and nature of reform to state power.

Some coalition elements emphasised liberal governance institutions and political pluralism, while others sought a redistribution of social and political power. The latter's initial optimism was soon tested. The 1987 Constitution, for example, enshrined the rights of 'marginalized sectors' – including workers, farmers, women, the urban poor, and the elderly – to be represented in local government. However, while this was mandated in the 1991 Local Government Code, resistance from traditional elites in Congress blocked required enabling law.

Oligarchic dominance of Congress was also promptly reasserted under President Corazon Aquino (1986–1992). Even electoral reform in 1995 through a new civil society expression MOP – the Party-List System meant to preserve 20 per cent of House of Representatives seats for marginalised sectors, organisations, and parties – was exploited by powerful elites to boost their influence, while also contributing to the further expansion of small, politically fragmented civil society groups. Singe-issue groups and particularist ideologies grew, including of gender, ethnicity, and indigeneity. Particularist ideologies of geography were integral to strategies by regional elite business and political clans to wins seats (see Rodan 2018: 121–8).

The most influential of radical reformers are also tied to the Akbayan Citizens' Action Party, a party-list organisation established in 1998 by leftists who withdrew from the NDF. In their conception of democracy and the strategy to overthrow oligarchic capitalism, the autonomy and integrity of CSOs and their engagement with the state through political parties is essential (Quimpo 2008: 90). By contrast, the CPP-NPA boycotted elections from 1986 until 2001.

The lack of cohesive and effective representation of the most socially and economically marginalised helps explain the 1998 election of the charismatic populist Joseph Estrada as president; his pro-poor and anti-oligarchy rhetoric won strong working-class support. In office, Estrada upset established oligarchs by favouring his own cronies through state patronage, while the Catholic Church hierarchy viewed his personal behaviour as morally objectionable, and middle-class NGO activists saw him as a threat to liberal governance. Following corruption allegations and EDSA 2 mobilisations, Estrada was removed by extra-constitutional means in 2001 legitimised by the Supreme Court, but he maintained enough working-class support for an EDSA 3 mobilisation that unsuccessfully sought his reinstatement.

In Gramscian terms, this taking down of a democratically elected president was the outcome of an historically specific crisis of political authority that threatened the interests – and the hegemony – of a dominant bloc of social forces in the Philippines. As Hedman (2006: 172) argued, this crisis 'stemmed from the newly self-evident dangers of elections themselves, as the popular – and quasi-populist – appeal of Estrada worked to overshadow, if not eliminate, the electoral power of money and machinery on which oligarchy was based'.

Estrada deviated from his post-Marcos presidential predecessors in generally bypassing policymaking consultation with CSOs – no less than with Congress – to challenge the positions of influential Filipino business and Catholic Church leaders and to marginalise assorted professional associations that had become increasingly linked with them since EDSA. To be sure, diverse elements outside the dominant bloc of interests joined the movement to oust Estrada, including from Bayan and Akbayan. This only underlined the success of dominant bloc interests in steering conflict away from overt class struggle to resolve the crisis of political authority (see Hedman 2006: 174–5).

4.3 Liberal Reformism and Its Limits

The Estrada scare nevertheless identified inequality as a problem for elite political management. This served as a spur for the societal incorporation MOP involving community-driven development (CDD) projects through joint anti-poverty initiatives of the Philippines government and multilateral agencies. Most significant of these was the Comprehensive and Integrated Delivery of Social Services (*Kalahi*-CIDSS) project involving the World Bank. Such projects incorporated individuals – but not representatives of collective organisations – into village-level consultative bodies, often in highly technical administrative deliberations. They were not designed to accommodate wider debate or contestation over the best ways to counter poverty. Consultation is founded on the premise that market-supportive instruments are essential to defeating poverty (Reid 2005, 2008).

Societal incorporation was taken to another level in 2010 with the election to president of the Liberal Party's Benigno Aquino III, whose campaign slogan was '*Kung walang corrupt, walang mahirap*' ('If there is no corruption, there will be no poverty'). Strengthening local participation was central to this strategy, within which his administration's bottom-up-budgeting (BUB) initiative starting in 2012 was pivotal.

For different reasons, BUB was advocated both by moderates within CODE-NGO and radicals aligned with Akbayan and leftist CSOs. The former looked to BUB to build public policy problem-solving capacity and deliver concrete project outcomes prior to elections. Radicals, by contrast, hoped BUB could increase the scope for political organisation and contestation over existing inequalities of power underpinning poverty and other social problems. Consequently, there were differences over who should be empowered, how much, and on what issues (see Rodan 2018: 147–53). These differences were embedded at high levels within the Aquino administration which included many 'crossovers': political actors with substantial civil society backgrounds (see Dressel 2012).

By late 2013, the entire country's 1,634 cities and municipalities had been invited to participate in BUB. The idea was that, by incorporating social actors into the budget cycle, patronage politics and corruption could be reduced to the benefit of projects serving genuinely local needs.

Alongside the Benigno Aquino administration's anti-corruption agenda conditional cash transfer spending was also boosted from US$254 million in 2010 to US$1.5 billion in 2014 (Kim and Yoo 2015: 84). This measure acknowledged that, despite a buoyant economy between 2003 and 2009, poverty increased from 24.5 per cent to 26.5 per cent (Kim and Yoo 2015: 79). Yet the conditional nature of the scheme was also a concession to a widespread perception among the middle class that poverty was the result of laziness and other behavioural weaknesses. The dismissal of structural factors reflected middle-class anxiety about their own prospects for material gains. These had become increasingly contingent on market dynamics as neoliberal policies continued to transform the Philippines' economy and society.

Importantly, oligarchs' search for profitable opportunities never leads to the sorts of state-led EOI programmes of Singapore or Malaysia. Easier avenues were available by virtue of the patron–client relations between business and state, including privatisations in the 1990s of utility, infrastructure, and energy sectors (Raquiza 2014). Ironically, subsequent opportunities in services and non-manufacturing industrial sectors fuelled by domestic consumption were founded on the repatriation of OFW funds. By 2017, there were 2.2 million OFWs whose US$28.1 billion remittances represented around 10 per cent of Philippines' GDP (Philippine Statistics Authority 2017; Cuaresma 2018).

However, while OFWs predominantly engage in manual work, their political and ideological orientations are complex. Hau (2017: 47) argues that, upon the receipt of remittances back in the Philippines, this rendered OFW 'family members part of the new middle class, with the wherewithal to send their children to school, purchase real estate in their hometown or regional cities and in the capital, and invest in small enterprises'. Duterte's emphasis on moral politics resonated with many of these OFWs, and with others in the middle-class unsupportive of large-scale redistributive policies to aid the poor.

Broadly, dynamic capital accumulation strategies in services and non-manufacturing sectors not only shaped coalitions of interest between different fractions of capital, public officials, and political elites. They also produced structural contexts for conflicts over poverty and inequality involving other social forces. The ideological mediation of such conflicts could – and did – result in cross-class support at the ballot box for populist candidates who rejected MOPs of societal incorporation and both consensus and democratic ideologies of participation.

Aquino's administration was unable to substantially arrest corruption, failed to pursue legislation to curb the dominance of Congress by political dynasties or significantly progress land reform, and made insufficient gains towards affordable and efficient public services. This opened the door again for a populist campaign against 'establishment politics'. As Bello (2017) discerned:

> 'By 2016, there was a yawning gap between the republic's promise of popular empowerment and wealth distribution and the reality of massive poverty, scandalous inequality, and pervasive corruption. The EDSA republican discourse of democracy, human rights, and the rule of law, had become a suffocating straightjacket for a majority of Filipinos, who simply could not relate to it owing to the overpowering reality of their powerlessness'
>
> (see also Thompson 2016).

In essence, class conflicts between different civil society forces that started to play out immediately after EDSA – and manifested in EDSA 2 and EDSA 3 – laid foundations for Duterte's rise to power. A new phase in the crisis of political authority and the hegemony of the dominant bloc of interests was now entered – some interests threatened, others not.

4.4 Duterte's Authoritarian Populism

Duterte was elected president in May 2016, with cross-class support including strong backing from the young and educated middle class, defeating an assortment of liberal and conservative parties and candidates (*ABS-CBN News* 2016). Previously mayor of Davao City in regional Philippines, Duterte's small party *Hugpong sa Tawong Lungsod* (People of the Towns Party) was unaligned with any major party. This resonated with his claim to offer a sharp break from establishment politics. As the supposedly authentic direct representative of 'the people', he would not be reliant on intermediary political institutions or encumbered by them.

The intermediary institution of BUB was thus an immediate casualty once Duterte was in office. He also used socialist with anti-oligarchic rhetoric during the election campaign, promising to address some left agendas (see Sanchez and

Lamchek 2021). Indeed, members of the NDF and CPP accepted offers of post-election cabinet-level positions on agricultural reform, social welfare, and anti-poverty programmes. Duterte also facilitated the release of high-level CPP military captives, initiating moves towards a final peace negotiation between the government and communist rebels.

However, the presence of leftists within the administration, as Duterte's extrajudicial killings in his war on drugs escalated, caused consternation among human rights activists – including within NDF ranks. This uncomfortable political position persisted for fifteen months, by which time Duterte demonstrated little commitment to land reform, environmental protection, labour contracting, or other left issues of inequality and poverty. His support for the transfer of the body of former dictator Marcos to the Philippine's Cemetery of Heroes in November 2017 was the final straw, given how despised Marcos was by the left. This precipitated the departure of NDF members from Cabinet and the abandonment of peace talks between the government and the CPP-NPA, now officially designated a terrorist group.

Duterte thereafter sought to boost his intra-state support bases in ways functional for further limiting space in civil society for opposition to, and scrutiny of, his exercise of power. This included extending the powers and resources of the police and military. Executive Order No. 70, for instance, reinforced the Armed Forces of the Philippines' (AFP) role through its Development Support and Security Plan *Kapayappan* to ensure the involvement of NGOs, CSOs, and POs in the national security agenda, under which 'red-tagging' of human rights defenders, lawyers, activists and Duterte critics escalated (CIHR 2020: 4). Being suspected – or even labelled – a member of the Communist Party of the Philippines could amount to a death sentence. Extrajudicial killings were estimated to be in the tens of thousands by mid-2020 (Ratcliffe 2020).

Social media were also increasingly harnessed in Duterte's use of state power to narrow the scope for civil society contestation. This included availing bloggers who identified as Diehard Duterte Supporters of access to consultancy contracts, and 'allowances' from the Presidential Communications Operations Office, which also set aside a budget for bloggers to monitor and influence online sentiment towards Duterte (Cabañes and Cornelio 2017; *Rappler* 2017).

Investigative journalists and broadcasters critical of Duterte's administration were targeted by these trolls and subjected to questionable legal and regulatory measures. This included a court case against Maria Ressa, editor of the online newspaper *Rappler*, and the closure of ABS-CBN, one of the Philippines leading televisions stations. Senator Leila de Lima, who initiated a Senate hearing into extrajudicial killings, was subsequently charged with drug trafficking and arrested – despite agents from the Philippine Drug Enforcement Agency and the Anti-Money Laundering Council testifying under oath that no evidence linked her to drug trafficking (Bello 2020).

At times, Duterte deployed state power to threaten and intimidate the minority of liberal-leaning individual oligarchs who incurred his wrath, while pro-Duterte oligarchs – known as *Dutertegarchs* – often reaped commercial benefits from these spats. Approval ratings for Duterte remained extremely high among the upper class, most business chambers, and groups expressing strong support for his governance – or avoiding public criticisms of it (Heydarian 2020).

While there was no reforming of oligarchic capitalism, Duterte's reshaping of state power through boosting the repressive arms of the state, eroding the independence of the judiciary, and intimidating independent critical media had profound implications for civil society expression. According to Thompson (2021), opposition came to be 'confined to the rump of the once powerful Liberal Party, a defensive Catholic Church hierarchy, a small urban intelligentsia and civil society activists'.

4.5 Civil Society Transformation

Duterte shied away from challenging the structural power of oligarchic capitalism, but state power was altered during his rule. He strengthened the repressive arms of the state and eroded the independence and capacity of judicial, regulatory, and media institutions to transform the extent and form of political opposition possible through formal and informal political spaces of civil society. Social forces supportive of Duterte through social media were incorporated into this project.

Social bases of CSOs of varying ideological complexions suffered under Duterte. Numerous state funded development programmes through which moderate and radical activists engaged on behalf of rural and urban poor communities were axed under Duterte (Lorch 2021: 91), including BUB. The NDF's initial cooperation with Duterte also weakened its legitimacy in many activists' eyes. Meanwhile, Akbayan's alignment with the Liberal Party, which failed to reform oligarchic capitalism under Aquino, posed questions about its future reform coalition strategies through civil society expression.

Even before Duterte came to office, the influence of the Catholic Bishops' Conference of the Philippines (CBCP) had begun to wane. Its opposition to the Reproductive Health Bill, for example, failed to dissuade the Congress, which passed the Bill in 2012 (Tawatao 2014). After initial divisions within the CBCP over Duterte, its cautious criticisms over extra-judicial killings were rejected and derided by the president (Timberman 2019). The Church's record on child sexual abuse was also highlighted by Duterte in his dismissal of its moral authority.

Whether Catholic Church leaders are casualties in a rationalisation of the dominant bloc of interests will become clearer under the new administration of President Ferdinand 'Bongbong' Marcos Jr – the son of the authoritarian former president, Ferdinand.

Marcos Jr's emphatic presidential victory in May 2022 was aided by an alliance with vice-presidential candidate, Sara Duterte-Carpio, the daughter of the outgoing president. Allies of the Marcos and Duterte families now enjoy a super majority ensuring legislative control and enhanced capacity to further reshape state power and institutions. Yet, intra-elite conflicts over control of state power cannot be ruled out in the coming years of this administration.

Crucially, oligarchic structural power appears likely to consolidate for the foreseeable future, which almost guarantees no resolution to long-standing problems of poverty, inequality, or corruption. This may test the ideological appeal of authoritarian populism. However, forging of coherent reformist alternatives remains challenging given divergent interests within civil society over capitalist models of development.

5 Capital, Monarchy, and Military: Thailand's Polarised Civil Society

Military and military-backed administrations have generally dominated power in Thailand since the end of absolute monarchy in 1932. The flicker of democratic politics was not extinguished, but only when the Cold War ended and capitalist development accelerated, did pressures for political liberalisation gather momentum. Thailand's watershed 1997 Constitution – the first drafted by an elected Constitutional Drafting Assembly – paved the way for a return to electoral politics after the 1991 coup. By 2006, though, a democratically elected government had been overthrown in yet another military coup – one supported, legitimised, and celebrated by anti-democratic forces in civil society. The process was repeated in 2014, ushering in comprehensive authoritarian state powers protecting an established oligarchy incorporating business, monarchy, and military interests.

Thailand's dramatic shifts towards and away from liberal democracy were also linked to another watershed – the 1997–1998 AFC. This helped generate new coalitions in civil society heightening conflicts over who should politically participate, how and on what. These conflicts were due to the success – *not failure* – of democratic representation, as elected governments between

2001–2006 and 2011–2014 advanced the interests of hitherto marginalised socio-economic groups and challenged some powers of the dominant bloc of interests. Liberal and conservative crafters and many supporters of the 1997 constitution had not anticipated this.

In Thailand, we see in starkest terms of all four countries, how mobilisation of forces through civil society expression in opposition to – and defence of – democratic elections links to sharply contrasting social, economic, and ideological interests over who politically controls capitalism and how its fruits and costs are distributed. Putting the democratic elections genie back in the bottle has been no simple matter, given support from Thailand's rural and urban poor for socially redistributive measures made possible through elections (see Glassman 2010).

The challenge has been as much ideological as political, something readily understood by traditional elites and aligned forces in civil society. Accordingly, they invoke particularist and consultative ideologies of representation emphasising special entitlements of urban elites in Bangkok, complemented by non-democratic moral ideologies of accountability and governance. This class struggle reflected a different mix and evolution of oligarchic elements accompanying capitalist development in Thailand from the Philippines.

In this struggle, social forces from the urban and rural poor combined with emerging business interests to pursue and defend a reformist agenda that was resisted and suppressed by established elites from the military, business, the monarchy, and the middle class.

5.1 State–Civil Society Foundations

Thailand's transition to capitalism did not terminate ideologies justifying the old order. At different stages in struggles over state power and capitalist development, aspects of these conservative ideologies would be harnessed, adapted, and/or supplemented by kings, aristocrats and other interests among the military, business, and actors in civil society.

Under Thailand's pre-capitalist use-value production system, the interests of kings and aristocrats were structurally aligned in a hierarchical *sakdina* system of graded social rankings distinguishing two essential classes: *phrai* and *that* (commoners and slaves) and the ruling class of *nai* (aristocrats), the former bound by laws to provide labour services (or pay taxes in lieu) to the latter. The king, in turn, relied upon his aristocracy and officials, who supplied their peasants for military and labour service, and for providing surpluses for royal trade. Ideological rationalisations for such arrangements combined Buddhism and monarchy (Hewison 1989: 35).

Against the backdrop of economic crises and depression, the 1932 Revolution ended centuries of absolutist royal rule and ushered in a new civilian democratic political regime riven by conflicts between conservative and radical factions. Led by the People's Party (*Khana Rasadom*), these factions coalesced on constitutionalism. However, former defence minister Prince Boworadet and royalist officers staged an armed revolt in the 1933 Boworadet Rebellion aimed at restoring absolute monarchy. Fighting lasted from 11 October to 23 October, but people rallied in support of the People's Party and government military forces prevailed.

Intense manoeuvring over state power ensued thereafter between politically powerful groups and class fractions (Hewison 1989: 61). By 1938, the military faction gained the upper hand within the People's Party, resulting in the appointment to prime minister of Army leader General Phibun. Military dominance of cabinet posts followed, as did media sloganeering rationalising Phibun's growing powers, new laws curbing press freedom, and an emergency decree with extensive arrest powers (Baker and Pasuk 2005: 126).[16] The shift to authoritarianism was even more decisive following a 1947 royalist-backed military coup. This was not only an assault on civilian rule, but one that its leaders underlined would 'respect the principles of Nation, Religion and King' (in Baker and Pasuk 2005: 142). They were also critical of the state-initiated push towards industrialisation under civilian government, projecting a renewed emphasis on the export of primary commodities and increased foreign investment (Hewison 1989: 77).

Yet it was with the coup led by General Sarit – who came to power in twin coups in 1957 and 1958 – that the People's Party's ideology and policies were buried as the monarchy became crucial to the ideological legitimacy of military rule. That year, *lése magestè* laws against insulting the king dating back to absolute monarchy were integrated into a new Criminal Code. Throughout the next three decades of the Cold War, under Sarit and his successors, US patronage of Thailand was utilised to accelerate capitalist development, strengthen dictatorship, and further embed the ideological importance of the monarchy (see Glassman 2020).

Meanwhile, opposition to capitalism, US imperialism and military dictatorship variously involved workers, peasants, students, and intellectuals (Baker and Pasuk 2005: 188, 197–8). Civil society expression was risky. Responses were often brutal, including a crackdown on student protesters on 6 October 1976, when police and right-wing, royalist, vigilantes killed more than 100 protesters at Thammasat University, alleging protesters were anti-monarchical communists

---

[16] Phibun was prime minister from 1938 to 1944, and again from 1948 to 1957.

(Solomon 2016). In the 1970s, union organisers and peasant leaders were assassinated.

Amidst the political ructions, a striking theme to Thai capitalism from early twentieth century to the 1980s was the mutually beneficial links between state and capital (Hewison 1989; see also Ukrist and Connors 2021). Through these ties, banking capital became the dominant fraction of capital and costs to capital were generally contained at the expense of peasants and workers. Veerayooth's (2018b: 256) study of post–World War II capitalism through to 1997 particularly linked contemporary inequality to the dominance of a 'group of royalist military', and a small circle of leading bankers and technocrats in policymaking who eschewed redistributive policies and programmes.

Importantly, Veerayooth (2018b: 264) also highlighted how policymaking favoured capital and *urban* workers over labour and *rural* workers. Indeed, inequalities in Thailand have one of the world's most exceptional spatial gradients, such is the concentration of economic growth in Bangkok (Glassman 2019: 305). The articulation between inequalities based on social class and region would form a powerful political cocktail in civil society polarisation in the years ahead.

5.2 Liberalisation, Economic Crisis, and New Coalitions

Economic liberalisation led to both an economic boom in the 1980s and accentu-ated income and wealth differentials – including along regional lines (Glassman 2019: 310). The end of the Cold War also gradually led to pressures for greater local and national political engagement (Hewison 2010: 120). This included Bloody May protests in 1992 against military rule, in which more than fifty protestors were killed. It also included the proliferation of organisations seeking policies to alleviate the negative social and environmental impacts of new or accelerated forms of economic development unleashed by neoliberalism.

The Community Organisation Development Institution (CODI) became an especially expansive and influential network of NGOs, boasting 12,000 organ-isations by 1989 (Kanokwan 2020: 367). Initially, these NGOs were supported by foreign donors but, when such sources dried up, closer ties with the state evolved – especially following the advent of the AFC. Indeed, the state now served as the 'cradle of financial and organisational resources', resulting in an increasing centralisation of CSOs (Veerayooth 2018a: 154).

Closer state–civil society cooperation led to societal incorporation MOP initiatives. Under the Social Investment Fund, for example, local farmers' and other NGO networks participated in the formulation and implementation of post-AFC rescue packages (Jayasuriya and Rodan 2007: 784). The influence of ideological approaches to development reinforcing the political authority of the monarchy was also extended. From the 1950s, Royally Initiated Projects drew on public, private, and royal funds to establish consultative networks across society and incorporating government departments (Chanida, Chaithawat, and Thanapol 2004: 99–101). During the AFC, the king promoted the 'self-sufficient economy', under which it is 'sufficient to live and to eat' (in Missingham 2003: 2). Such initiatives pushed CSOs into division over their relationship to the monarchy.

Independent rural grassroots organisations also emerged from 1990, including the Small Scale Farmers' Assembly of Isan in the north of Thailand, which protested about land rights and other concerns. In 1997, the Assembly of the Poor staged a ninety-nine-day protest in Bangkok too. Meanwhile, agricultural commercialisation in Isan in the north led to widening disparities in farmers' incomes, alongside the spread of new communication technologies enabling collective awareness and action (Somchai 2016: 139–46).

The AFC left many domestic capitalists in disarray (see Pasuk and Baker 2008). It also facilitated the political rise of business tycoon Thaksin Shinawatra, whose profitable investments in private broadcasting media and telecommunications were made possible by economic deregulation beginning in the 1980s. The cash flows from these investments enabled Thaksin to withstand the AFC and establish and lead a party under the new constitution, founding the *Thai Rak Thai* (Thais Love Thais, or *TRT*) party in 1998. *TRT* was initially conceived as 'a vehicle to represent the interests of domestic capital and to rebuild, reshape and support this class' (Hewison 2010: 123).

Thaksin also forged links with pro-poor NGOs as well as 1970s 'Octoberist' student activists who contributed to *TRT* policymaking (Hewison 2010: 124). His encouragement of farmers to join the market economy to advance their economic and social interests sharply contrasted with the paternalist rural development strategies of self-sufficiency championed by the king, which many CODI organisations aligned with (Veerayooth 2018a: 162). This contrast would assume major importance in electoral politics. As Glassman (2011: 39) observed, hard work, limited consumerism and respect for nation, religion and king were supposedly the appropriate paths to merit and a better life, but the 'TRT harnessed this subordination to royalist and nationalist hegemony and inadvertently transformed it into a force that challenges that hegemony'.

TRT incorporated elements of business, the middle class, workers, and the rural poor on a platform of economic nationalism, welfarism and the rejection of IMF austerity as a response to the AFC (Hewison 2006). It came to office in 2001, leading a three-party coalition controlling 325 lower house seats out of a possible 500. In the 2005 election, *TRT* achieved a landslide victory in its own right, taking 376 seats. Signature policies underpinning *TRT*'s electoral landslides included support for farmers and local business, broad anti-poverty programmes, and a universal healthcare system. Labelled 'populist', these policies inspired claims of corruption and 'electoral majoritarianism', the wider business community and the urban middle class seeking a return to the pre-AFP social order, and especially to the poor having to fend for themselves.

Conflicting agendas between Thaksin and his critics precipitated the emergence of a deep social divide, two military coups, and protracted political and constitutional crises – reflecting competing preferences for which MOPs should mediate conflict and how.

5.3 Forces in Civil Society: For and Against Democracy

The 1997 constitution was a largely elite project principally to transcend the political fragmentation and corruption of parliamentary politics in the 1990s, rather than to foster egalitarianism (Veerayooth 2018a: 160). For example, parliamentary candidates were now required to hold a university degree, effectively barring workers and poor farmers. And while the constitution was designed to facilitate a stronger executive and parliamentary system, the substantive ends to which executive and party power were put under Thaksin – including both social redistribution and the undermining of horizontal accountability – alarmed both conservatives and liberals. When Thaksin sold his family's shares in telecommunications company Shin Corporation to the Singapore GLC Temasek Holdings in 2006 – a US$1.9 billion transaction which allowed Thaksin and his family to avoid capital gains tax – political polarisation and social division reached boiling point.

Over the next sixteen years, contending mass mobilisations unfolded, including protests and campaigns by the: People's Alliance for Democracy (PAD) and the 'Yellow Shirts' movement in 2006 and 2008; United Front for Democracy Against Dictatorship (UDD) and the 'Red Shirts' movement protests in 2009 and 2010; People's Democratic Reform Committee (PDRC), the successor to the PAD, in 2013–2014; and the People's Party movement in 2020–2021. This was a struggle over the margins of contestation permissible through the civil society expression MOP.

During election campaigning in 2001, Thaksin emphasised his non-establishment credentials as a self-made business tycoon from humble rural beginnings (Pasuk and Baker 2009: 84–5), but populism was not his defining ideological position. Initially, he engaged with various intermediary groups – labour in particular – before dissatisfaction with this led down technocratic administrative incorporation paths (see Brown 2007: 826–30). However, support for Thaksin and *TRT*'s redistributive policies led to thematic charges of populism to discredit this agenda in the lead up to the 2006 military coup. For Thaksin's elite and middle-class opponents – who had benefited so much from the pre-1997 economic boom – social redistribution was 'buying votes' (see Thanasak and Gethin 2019: 7).

It was only with the advent of the Red Shirt movement that Thaksin was manoeuvred into becoming populist through the combined circumstances of 'elite opposition, political exile,[17] violence and the loss of access to electoral politics' (Hewison 2019: 427). He began linking his struggle and that of his people as one for 'true democracy' against an identifiable 'other' of a Bangkok-based elite (Hewison 2019: 434). In sharp contrast with Duterte in the Philippines, Thaksin was a circumstantial populist whose policies had precipitated a concerted backlash from powerful vested interests.

Crucially, the removal of Thaksin in the 2006 coup and the forced dissolution of *TRT* was not enough to suppress the appetite among marginalised Thais for electoral representation. Hence, pro-Thaksin parties secured emphatic electoral victories in 2007 and 2011 and were among the most successful in 2019 in the first elections following the 2014 military coup.

Various CSOs and their middle-class leaders campaigned with royalists, the military, the elitist judiciary, and right-wing groups to overturn electoral outcomes. Opposing this was the UDD, which was pro-Thaksin and mainly supported by workers and small farmers. Class antagonisms were most evident when the UDD mobilised around issues of inequality, injustice, and opposition to an 'aristocratic elite' (Kengkij and Hewison 2009; Hewison 2010). Meanwhile, middle-class-led organisations eschewed class politics in favour of governance issues such as corruption (see Chomthongdi and Chanida 2010).

PAD encompassed professional, business, student, and religious organisations, as well as individual members of the urban middle class (Veerayooth 2018a: 163). One PAD camp included urban elites and conservatives such as royalist civil servants marginalised under *TRT*, as well as elements of business bypassed under Thaksin's patronage system. Another involved social movements and NGOs with grassroot bases incorporating state enterprise workers, farmers, teachers, and students (Pye and Schaffar 2008: 40). Some Octoberists concerned about Thaksin's authoritarianism were in this second camp.

CODI and its network were prominent in 2006 mobilisations against Thaksin, whose policies favouring commercialised farming severed traditional links

---

[17] Thaksin left Thailand after the 2006 coup.

between farmers, civil society, and state (Jayasuriya and Hewison 2004: 575). Thaksin's policies also challenged paternalistic ideological notions of a 'communitarian democracy' which rationalised CODI's development roles. Such a 'democracy', according to one of its leading advocates, the royalist Prawase Wasi, is grounded in Buddhist teaching emphasising community members working together in a 'morally superior' version of democracy, compared with the West (Thorn 2017: 157).

This religious-nationalist worldview combines elements of particularist and consultative ideologies of political representation to conceal hierarchical power relationships and conflicts thereof – especially class conflicts. Similar claims about the centrality of moral authority to political rule and a culturally authentic approach to democracy were made by others supportive of PAD. According to Hewison and Kengkij (2010: 188), this 'Thai-style Democracy' transforms citizens into 'children-people' on whose behalf the elite make decisions. Essentially, for PAD, only 'good' people should be entrusted with political power and governance, and elections are dangerous because the 'uneducated' and 'stupid' can be duped to support 'bad' people (see Glassman 2019: 311).

Such profoundly elitist ideology was different from the elitist republicanism of the PAP in Singapore. It was in defence of an old social order founded on aristocratic and monarchical power, not the basis of a new – albeit also authoritarian – technocratic state capitalist order.

Hence, despite earlier rhetoric, PAD and Yellow Shirt members did not look to principles of constitutionalism to advance their calls for Thaksin's removal. As early as February 2006, PAD leader and media mogul Sondhi Limthongkul appealed to the king to remove Thaksin from power (Pasuk and Baker 2011: 90). PAD also called for a 'new politics' centred on the moral authority of the king, which gave increasing clarity to the undemocratic nature of accountability, governance, and citizenship PAD endorsed (see Sinpeng 2021: 130–1).

The Red Shirt movement initially formed in opposition to the 2007 military-backed constitution, which was headed for a referendum. It had a strong regional and ethnic foundation in the communities of Isan and northern Thailand, where pro-Thaksin parties had enjoyed support (Glassman 2019: 311). Red Shirts also encompassed broader civic groups, including some Thaksin critics who had abandoned PAD.[18] Red Shirt mobilisations utilised People's Television talk shows and rallies (Sinpeng 2021: 149; see also Sopranzetti 2020: 157–61). The biggest demonstrations against military rule followed the seizure by the Supreme Court of US$1.4 billion of Thaksin's assets in 2010. A planned seven-day rally

---

[18] Among these were Octobersist who had aligned with PAD out of opposition to Thaksin's authoritarianism and who opposed PAD's royalism and anti-electoral politics.

escalated to sixty-four days involving more than a million Red Shirt supporters. Authorities responded violently, resulting in ninety-one deaths and over 2,000 injured (Sinpeng 2021: 149).

By this time, the sense of systematic class and other discrimination against the marginalised had become a politically powerful ingredient to the Red Shirt movement, fuelled by double standards in the exercise of law and judicial inconsistencies (see Rodan and Hughes 2014: 174). There would be no account- ability for the 2010 killings. Particularist ideologies of ethnicity, geography, religion, and culture by Yellow Shirts to rationalise elitist alternatives to elect- oral democracy were equally provocative and politically galvanising for Red Shirts. This included racist-classist terms like 'water buffalo' to portray Red Shirt villagers (Glassman 2019: 311).

The apparent success of the 2006 military coup was eventually followed by a 2011 election which delivered government to the newly formed *Pheu Thai Party* headed by Yinluck Shinawatra – Thaksin's sister. Those who had sup- ported PAD reformed as the PDRC in late 2013. It was led by the opposition Democratic Party but incorporated PAD networks and leaders (see McCargo and Naruemon 2021: 127).

The PDRC's objective was to bring down the elected, pro-Thaksin govern- ment, with early calls for the military to intervene. Opposing Yingluck meant thwarting the 'majoritarianism' of elections – including by violence and intimi- dation. In short, 'reform' meant a new constitution that would ensure the sovereign will of the people did not principally determine election outcomes (see Prajak 2016). According to Sinpeng (2021: 150), the PDRC was more ideologically radical and anti-democratic than the PAD. This was also the 'first mass digitally mediated movement in Thailand', far more effective is harness- ing social media than Red Shirts because of class: 'Thais who were more urbanized, more educated, and more wealthy were more likely to be active users of social media' (Sinpeng 2021: 154).

The significance of class for political polarisation and mobilisation warrants elaboration. By 2016, Thailand's income inequality was amongst the highest in the world, the top 10 per cent receiving 53 per cent of national income. Yet, between 2001 and 2016, inequalities decreased slightly between both Thai citizens and regions. This was due to policies of the Thaksin and Yingluck governments between 2001 and 2014, translating into strong electoral support among low-income and lower-educated voters (see Thanasak and Gethin 2019).

Meanwhile, extreme concentrations of incomes and wealth also ensured that traditional elites – including the established middle class – consolidated their prosperity. The position of the emerging middle class from humble social and regional backgrounds, by contrast, was not cushioned by wealth but more dependent on income and public goods. Accordingly, Thanasak and Gethin (2019: 8) characterise the respective demonstrations by Yellow and Red Shirts as not just a clash between rich and poor, but also between the emerging and established middle class – the former more supportive of democratic elections, the latter readily aligning with powerful traditional elites.

Against the background of the PDRC's successful mobilisation resulting in a military coup, repression against their online critics intensified, not just through sedition and defamation laws but escalating use of the *lèse magesté* law. Intimidation and trolling also involved groups with such menacing names as Social Sanction and Rubbish Collection Organisation, the Network of Volunteer Citizens to Protect Monarchy on Facebook, and the Anti-Ignorance Association. These were just the latest in Thailand's long history of vigilantes and anti-democratic forces in civil society linking with the state to intimidate regime critics (see Bowie 1997: 107–10; Janjira 2021).

5.4 Elections Still 'Unsafe'

Military rule was considered necessary by anti-democratic and liberal forces at numerous points in Thailand's history, but a return to 'safe' elections was also regarded as an optimal direction at the appropriate time. Elections were thus reintroduced in March 2019. However, under the new constitution drawn up under a military junta, the prime minister was to be chosen by a parliament including all 250 members of the Senate appointed by the junta. This paved the way for General Prayut Chan-o-cha to continue at the helm as leader of the new *Palang Pracharath* (People's State) party, formed by fellow junta members.

Nevertheless, the pro-Thaksin *Pheu Thai* Party secured more constituency seats than *Palang Pracharath*. The youth-dominated progressive and social democratic newcomer Future Forward Party also polled well. In February 2020, the constitutional court dissolved it and imposed a ten-year ban from politics on its executive members. Yet the court's actions laid foundations for the emergence of a movement linked to the formation of the People's Party (adopting the name of the earlier republican party). This involved scores of rallies, including on 24 June 2020 – the anniversary of the overthrow of absolute monarchy – to demand the prime minister's resignation, constitutional changes, and reform of the monarchy. At a rally two months later, students raised questions about human rights violations and massive Crown Property Bureau's (CPB) assets (Penchan 2021).[19]

---

[19] These assets were conservatively estimated at US$70 billion in 2019, making Thai royals among the richest in the world (Hewison 2021: 264).

Intersections between these demands and Red Shirt agendas included attacks on wealth and power concentrations and rejections of nationalist ideology of authentic 'Thainess'. Hence, former Red Shirt leaders endorsed this movement (see Saowanee 2021). However, this movement called for monarchy reforms, directly challenging the *ancien* regime of monarchy-business-military, and a redress of inequalities encompassing not just class and locality, but also gender, age, and other forms of marginalisation (Pasit 2020). Particularist ideologies of representation were now harnessed in a claim for a more inclusive democracy.

According to Penchan (2021), this younger generation movement was 'energised by influences from a diverse set of online communities that have grown politicised – from pop culture fan clubs, LGBTQI+ groups, and YouTube celebrities' subscribers'. Hewison (2020) observed that 'the demonstrators have changed the way that the monarchy is considered and discussed'.

In contrast with the Red Shirts who had an organisational base in the UDD, this movement comprised several independent collective organisations with multiple interests. This was another element to the transformation of civil society in Thailand.

Predictably, anti-democratic forces also mobilised through civil society in opposition to this movement, whose momentum was hampered by COVID-19 and the arrest and indefinite detention – mostly under *lèse magesté* – of movement leaders (Janjira 2021). The severity of repression reflected the growing strength of popular rejection of monarchical and religious-nationalist worldviews as a rationale for limiting the political participation and influence of marginalised communities.

Ironically, this rejection grew not out of communist influence, but the social and political contradictions of successful capitalist development following the Cold War. This laid social foundations for conflicts and political alliances facilitating Thaksin's rise to power and the subsequent emergence of Red Shirt and People's Party movements. In the process, preferred MOPs among contending social forces have become both ideologically clearer and more hotly contested.

6 Conclusion

What has the MOP political economy framework revealed about the nature and direction of civil society in these four countries? What are the implications for understanding political regime directions more generally in Southeast Asia?

The framework steered analysis away from liberal normative and theoretical assumptions about civil society towards an attempt to understand relationships *within* and *between* civil society and state. Analytical emphasis on the dynamic social foundations and contradictions of capitalism was accompanied by concepts of non-democratic and democratic ideology to help explain when, why, and how different civil society forces compete or cooperate to reform, transform, or defend state power.

Capitalist dynamics and related conflicts have fostered new coalitions *within* and across civil society, as well as *between* actors in the political space of civil society and the state. These coalitions are often conservative or reactionary. Nevertheless, reformist forces have had their moments of opportunity – or seemed poised to – which is precisely why civil society struggles over state power have become so polarised in most of the cases examined.

The cases of Malaysia and Thailand emphatically illustrated this point. Forces in civil society with contrasting reform agendas helped bring about momentous changes of government, followed by counter civil society mobilisations opposed to projected liberal reforms in Malaysia, and implemented social democratic reforms in Thailand. In both cases, particularist ideologies were pivotal to these counter civil society mobilisations in support of established elite interests.

Class conflict was at play in both struggles, but in Thailand so was class consciousness among forces supporting socially redistributive programmes. This rendered the struggle between democratic and particularist ideologies in Thailand even more intense. Accelerated and transformative impacts of capitalist development in Thailand heightened popular awareness and resentment about acutely uneven social and regional benefits from it. This was galvanised and fostered through the historic coalition of forces in civil society aligned with the *TRT* and counter forces reacting to it through civil society.

Meanwhile, we saw how poverty and inequality in the Philippines have coexisted with extensive CSOs and a long history of democratic elections. Private oligarchic capitalism has contributed to these maladies through accumulation strategies. Oligarchs have also harnessed private resources and networks with state allies to block reformist agendas of liberal, social democratic, and socialist orientation. This has created periodic opportunities for populist ideologies and leaders to shape or control state power, bypassing civil society altogether and/or mobilising select anti-democratic forces in civil society through strategies of state repression against liberal and democratic forces in civil society.

A distinctive political economy was also integral to explaining why reformist forces in civil society have been most stunted in Singapore. Technocratic state capitalism rationalised by the ruling PAP's elitist ideology of meritocracy has fuelled tensions over social and material inequalities. Yet the economic and political resources at the disposal of a politico-bureaucratic class have also consolidated and extended with capitalist development. In the process, interests aligned with the PAP's ideology of meritocracy have been drawn into supportive relationships with the state, including through cultural and regulatory institutions and new MOPs promoting non-democratic consultative ideologies.

The exceptional ideological and political cohesion of the PAP's technocratic one-party state has facilitated systematic co-option, intimidation, and fragmentation of civil society forces in Singapore. Under Malaysian state capitalism, by contrast, different power relationships and ideological rationalisations apply. Intra-elite patronage struggles thus periodically open-up opportunities for strategic political coalitions by reformist forces – especially between CSOs and political parties – conspicuously absent in Singapore.

Clearly, distinctive political economies are crucial to explaining contrasting state–civil society relationships across authoritarian regimes – and indeed all regimes. Moreover, while neoliberalism has resulted in greater social and material inequalities in all cases, the precise complexion of political coalitions and ideologies brought into contest reflect contrasting political economies. Crucially, as the Thailand case most dramatically illustrates, when reformist forces act collectively through civil society to push for a more egalitarian society in opposition to powerful interests and elitist ideologies, this can ignite a brutal counter-reaction from forces within civil society in defence of an established order.

Far from undergoing a general retreat in Southeast Asia, increased activism through formal and informal civil society spaces is, in varying combinations, evident in much of the region and pivotal in shaping political regimes. This activism is pushing in both authoritarian and democratic directions, something that the political economy framework adopted here explains. Not only can this framework be applied to any country in Southeast Asia, but to the analysis of civil society everywhere to better understand dynamic struggles over state power shaping political regime directions.

Abbreviations and Acronyms

AFP	Armed Forces of the Philippines
AFC	Asian financial crisis
AMP	Association of Muslim Professionals
AWARE	Association of Women for Action and Research
BN	*Barisan Nasional* (National Front)
BS	*Barisan Sosialis* (Socialist Front)
BUB	bottom-up-budgeting
CODE-NGO	Caucus of Development Non-governmental Organizations
CSO	civil society organisation
CDD	community-driven development
CODI	Community Organisation Development Institution
CPP	Communist Party of the Philippines (*Partido Komunista ng Pilipinas*)
Kalahi-CIDSS	Comprehensive and Integrated Delivery of Social Services
CPB	Crown Property Bureau
DAP	Democratic Action Party
EC	Electoral Commission
EOI	export-oriented industrialisation
FU	Feedback Unit
Bersih	*Gabungan Philihanraya Bersih dan Adil* (Coalition for Clean and Fair Elections)
GLCs	government-linked companies
HOME	Humanitarian Organisation for Migration Economics
ISMA	*Ikatan Muslimin Malaysia* (Malaysian Muslim Solidarity)
ICERD	International Convention on the Elimination of All Forms of Racial Discrimination
ICC	International Criminal Court
IKRAM	*Pertubuhan Ikram Malaysia*
LGBTQI+	Lesbian, Gay, Bisexual, Transgender, Queer, and Intersex Life
MCA	Malayan Chinese Association
MIC	Malayan Indian Congress
MTUC	Malaysian Trades Union Congress
1MDB	1Malaysia Development Berhad
MEA	Ministry of Economic Affairs
MOM	Ministry of Manpower

MOP	mode of participation
NECC	National Economic Consultative Council
NDF	National Democratic Front
NTUC	National Trades Union Congress
NSS	Nature Society of Singapore
NEP	New Economic Policy
NPA	New Patriotic Alliance (*Bagong Alyansang Makabayan*)
NMP	nominated members of parliament
NGO	non-governmental organisation
OSC	Our Singapore Conversation
OFW	overseas foreign worker
PH	*Pakatan Harapan* (Coalition of Hope)
Amanah	*Parti Amanah Negara* (National Trust Party)
PAS	*Parti Islam Se-Malaysia* (Pan-Malaysian Islamic Party)
PKN	*Parti Keadilan Nasional* (National Justice Party)
PKR	*Parti Keadilan Rakyat* (People's Justice Party)
PPBM	*Parti Pribumi Bersatu Malaysia* (Malaysia United Indigenous Party)
Pekida	*Pertubuhan Kebajikan dan Dakwah Islamiyah SeMalaysia* (Association of Islamic Welfare and Dakwah of Malaysia)
PAP	People's Action Party
PAD	People's Alliance for Democracy
PDRC	People's Democratic Reform Committee
PLU	People Like Us
PO	people's organisation
PN	*Perikatan Nasional* (National Alliance)
POFMA	Protection from Online Falsehoods and Manipulation Act
PR	*Pakatan Rakyat*
REACH	Reaching Everyone for Active Citizenship @ Home
TRT	*Thai Rak Thai* (Thais Love Thais)
TWC2	Transient Workers Count Too
UEC	United Examination Certificate
UDD	United Front for Democracy Against Dictatorship
UMNO	United Malays National Organisation
UM	University of Malaya
VWO	voluntary welfare organisation
WP	Workers' Party

References

Abinales, P. and D. Amoroso. (2005). *State and Society in the Philippines*. Lanham, MD: Rowman & Littlefield.

ABS-CBN News (2016). 'More Millennials Voted for Deterte, Exit Polls Show', 14 May. https://news.abs-cbn.com/halalan2016/focus/05/14/16/more-millennials-voted-for-duterte-exit-poll-show.

Afiq, A. (2020). 'Happy New Year, Yellow Malays', *Malaysiakini*, 1 January. www.malaysiakini.com/letters/505519.

Alagappa, M. (2004). 'Civil Society and Political Change: An Analytical Framework'. In *Civil Society and Political Change in Asia: Expanding and Contracting Democratic Space*, M. Alagappa (ed.). Stanford, CA: Stanford University Press, pp. 25–60.

Almond, G. and S. Verba. (1963). *The Civic Culture, Political Attitudes and Democracy in Five Nations*. Newbury Park, CA: Sage.

Amoroso, D. J. (2014). *Traditionalism and the Ascendancy of the Malay Ruling Class in Colonial Malaya*. Singapore: NUS Press.

Anderson, P. (1976). 'The Antinomies of Antonio Gramsci', *New Left Review*, 100: 5–78.

Armony, A. (2004). *The Dubious Link: Civic Engagement and Democratization*. Stanford, CA: Stanford University Press.

Aspinall, E. (2004). 'Indonesia: Transformation of Civil Society and Democratic Breakthrough'. In *Civil Society and Political Change in Asia: Expanding and Contracting Democratic Space*, M. Alagappa (ed.). Stanford, CA: Stanford University Press, pp. 25–60.

Aspinall, E., D. Fossati, B. Muhtadi, and E. Warburton. (2020). 'Elites, Masses and Democratic Decline in Indonesia', *Democratization*, 27(4): 505–26.

Augustin, R. (2019). 'Unhappy with PH's GLC Appointments, NGOs Want Task Force for Reforms', *Free Malaysia Today*, 24 January. www.freemalaysiatoday.com/category/nation/2019/01/24/unhappy-with-phs-glc-appointments-ngos-want-task-force-for-reforms/?__cf_chl_jschl_tk__=pmd_z559cs WdZ81y4puiqRBpM2lU.iviirRDztjpSIQXGaA-1631698205-0-gqNtZGz NApCjcnBszQfR.

Baker, C. and P. Pasuk. (2005). *A History of Thailand*. Cambridge: Cambridge University Press.

Bal, C. S. (2016). *Production Politics and Migrant Labour Regimes: Guest Workers in Asia and the Gulf*. London: Palgrave Macmillan.

Barr, M. D. (2010). 'Marxists in Singapore? Lee Kuan Yew's Campaign Against Catholic Social Justice Activists in the 1980s', *Critical Asian Studies*, 42(3): 335–62.

(2014a). *The Ruling Elite of Singapore: Networks of Power and Influence.* London: I. B. Tauris.

(2014b). 'Singapore's Impotent Immigration Policy', *East Asia Forum*, 2 April. www.eastasiaforum.org/2014/04/02/singapores-impotent-immigration-policy/.

(2019). *Singapore: A Modern History.* London: I. B. Tauris.

Bello, W. (2017). 'Rodrigo Duterte: A Fascist Original', *Foreign Policy in Focus*, 6 January. https://fpif.org/rodrigo-duterte-fascist-original/ https://fpif.org/rodrigo-duterte-fascist-original/.

(2020). 'Statement of Walden Bello for "From Repression to Resistance," an Online Event Expressing Support for Freedom of the Press, Nov 21, 2020', *Campaign for Human Rights Philippines*, 22 November. http://chrp.org.uk/2020/statement-of-walden-bello-for-from-repression-to-resistance-an-online-event-expressing-support-for-freedom-of-the-press-nov-21-2020/.

Berman, S. (1997). 'Civil Society and the Collapse of the Weimar Republic', *World Politics*, 49(3): 401–29.

Bermeo, N. (2016). 'On Democratic Backsliding', *Journal of Democracy*, 27 (1): 5–19.

Bernhard, M. (1993). 'Civil Society and Democratic Transition in East Central Europe', *Political Science Quarterly*, 108(2): 307–26.

Blakkarly, J. (2015). 'Yellow Protesters Unafraid Calling for PM's Resignation', *Al Jazeera*, 30 August. www.aljazeera.com/features/2015/8/30/yellow-protesters-unafraid-calling-for-pms-resignation.

Bowie, K. (1997). *Rituals of National Identity: An Anthropology of the State and the Village Scout Movement in Thailand.* New York: Columbia University Press.

Braunstein, J. (2019). *Capital Choices: Sectoral Politics and the Variation of Sovereign Wealth.* Ann Arbor, MI: Michigan University Press.

Brook, T. (1997). 'Auto-organization in Chinese Society'. In *Civil Society in China*, T. Brook and B. M. Frolic (eds.). Armonk, NY: M. E. Sharpe, pp. 19–45.

Brown, A. (2007). 'Labour and Modes of Participation in Thailand', *Democratization*, 14(5): 816–33.

Cabãnes, J. and J. Cornelio. (2017). 'The Rise of Trolls in the Philippines (And What We Can Do About It)'. In *A Duterte Reader: Critical Essays on Rodrigo Duterte Early Presidency*, N. Curato (ed.). Quezon City: Ateneo de Manila Press, pp. 231–50.

Carnoy, M. (1984). *The State and Political Theory.* Princeton, NJ: Princeton University Press.

Carothers, T. (ed.). (2004). *Critical Mission: Essays on Democracy Promotion.* Washington, DC: Carnegie Endowment for International Peace.

Carroll, T. (2010). *Delusions of Development: The World Bank and the Post-Washington Consensus in Southeast Asia.* Basingstoke: Palgrave Macmillan.

Case, W. (2002). *Politics in Southeast Asia: Democracy More or Less.* London: Curzon.

Center for International Human Rights (CIHR). (2020). 'The Closing of Civil Space in the Philippines'. Submission to the OHCHR for HRC Report 41/2. John Jay College of Criminal Justice, City University of New York.

Chan, C. K. (1985). 'Eugenics on the Rise: A Report from Singapore', *International Journal of Health Services*, 15(4): 707–12.

Chanida, C., T. Chaithawat, and E. Thanapol. (2004). 'The Thai Monarchy and Non-Governmental Organisations'. In *The NGO Way: Perspectives and Experiences From Thailand*, S. Shigetomi, T. Kasian, and T. Apichart (eds.). Chiba-shi: Institute of Developing Economies, pp. 99–146.

Chin, J. (2019). 'Setting the Stage for Race-Baiting in Malaysia', *Malaysiakini*, 19 October. www.malaysiakini.com/news/496514.

Chomthongdi, J.-C. and C. Chanida. (2010). 'Aftermath of the Battle: Picking Up the Pieces', *Focus on the Global South*, 29 May. https://focusweb.org/aftermath-of-the-battle-picking-up-the-pieces/.

Chong, T. (2010). 'The State and the New Society: The Role of the Arts in Singapore Nation-building', *Asian Studies Review*, 34(2): 131–49.

Chua, B.-H. (1994). 'Arrested Development: Democratization in Singapore', *Third World Quarterly*, 15(4): 655–68.

(1997). *Political Legitimacy and Housing: Stakeholding in Singapore.* London: Routledge.

Chua, L. J. (2014). *Mobilizing Gay Singapore: Rights and Resistance in an Authoritarian State.* Singapore: NUS Press.

Chun, H. W. (2013a). 'In Singapore, Calls for Poverty Line Amid Rising Inequality', *Wall Street Journal*, 11 November. http://blogs.wsj.com/searealtime/2013/11/11/in-singapore-calls-for-poverty-line-amid-rising-inequality.

(2013b). 'Singaporeans Protest Immigration Plans', *Wall Street Journal*, 16 February. www.wsj.com/articles/SB10001424127887324616604578308222594086686.

Clutterbuck, R. (1973). *Riot and Revolution in Singapore and Malaya, 1945–63.* London: Faber & Faber.

Cohen, J. L. and A. Arato. (1992). *Civil Society and Political Theory.* Cambridge, MA: MIT Press.

Community for Advocacy and Political Education (CAPE). (2019). 'Case Study #4: Bukit Brown Cemetery', 20 November. https://sg.news.yahoo .com/over-1-000-people-at-returnourcpf-protest-at-hong-lim-park-093133980.html.

Croissant, A. and J. Haynes (eds.). (2021). 'Democratic Regression in Asia', Special Issue, *Democratization*, 28(1).

Cuaresma, B. (2018). 'OFW Remittances Hit \$28.1 Billion in 2017', *Business Mirror*, 15 February. https://businessmirror.com.ph/2018/02/15/ofw-remit tances-hit-28-1-billion-in-2017/.

Curato, N. (2016). 'Politics of Anxiety, Politics of Hope: Penal Populism and Duterte's Rise to Power', *Journal of Current Southeast Asian Affairs*, 35 (3): 91–109.

Deyo, F. C. (1981). *Dependent Development and Industrial Order: An Asian Case Study.* New York: Praeger.

de Dios, E. and P. Hutchcroft. (2003). 'Political Economy'. In *The Philippine Economy: Development, Politics and Challenges*, A. M. Baliscan and H. Hill (eds.). New York: Oxford University Press, pp. 45–73.

Diamond, L. (2002). 'Thinking About Hybrid Regimes', *Journal of Democracy*, 13(2): 21–35.

(2016). *In Search of Democracy.* Abingdon: Routledge.

Dressel, B. (2012). 'Targeting the Public Purse: Advocacy Coalitions and Public Finance in the Philippines', *Administration and Society*, 44(6 supplementary): 65s–84s.

Du Bois, C. (1962). *Social Forces in Southeast Asia.* Cambridge, MA: Harvard University Press.

Edwards, M. (2011). 'Conclusion: Civil Society as a Necessary and Necessarily Contested Idea'. In *The Oxford Handbook of Civil Society*, M. Edwards (ed.). Oxford: Oxford University Press, pp. 480–92.

(2020). *Civil Society.* 4th ed. Oxford: Polity Press.

Ehrenberg, J. (1999). *Civil Society: The Critical History of an Idea.* New York: New York University Press.

Eley, G. (2002). *Forging Democracy: The History of the Left in Europe, 1850–2000.* Oxford: Oxford University Press.

Emmerson, M. S. and J. S. Lamchek. (2021). 'The Year of Daring: Revisiting the Philippine Left's Dalliance with a Strongman', *Melbourne Asia Review*, 2 June. https://melbourneasiareview.edu.au/the-year-of-daring-revisiting-the-philippine-lefts-dalliance-with-a-strongman/.

Florini, A. (ed.). (2000). *The Third Force: The Rise of Transnational Civil Society*. Washington, DC: Japan Center for International Exchange and the Carnegie Endowment for International Peace.

Fukuyama, F. (1989). 'The End of History?', *The National Interest*, 16 (Summer): 3–18.

Geddie, J. (2020), 'Singapore's Fake New Law Trips up Opposition as Election Looms'. *Reuters*, 6 July. www.reuters.com/article/us-singapore-election-fakenews-idUSKBN2470NW

Glassman, J. (2010). '"The Provinces Elect Governments, Bangkok Overthrows Them": Urbanity, Class and Post-Democracy in Thailand', *Urban Studies*, 47(6): 1301–23.

(2011). 'Cracking Hegemony in Thailand: Gramsci, Bourdieu and the Dialectics of Rebellion', *Journal of Contemporary Asia*, 41(1): 25–46.

(2018). *Drums of War, Drums of Development: The Formation of a Pacific Ruling Class and Industrial Transformation in East and Southeast Asia, 1945–1980*. Leiden: Brill.

(2019). 'Class, Race, and Uneven Development in Thailand'. In *Routledge Handbook of Contemporary Thailand*, C. Pavin (ed.). London: Routledge, pp. 305–17.

(2020). 'Lineages of the Authoritarian State in Thailand: Military Dictatorship, Lazy Capitalism and the Cold War Past as Post-Cold War Prologue', *Journal of Contemporary Asia*, 50(4): 571–92.

Goh, C. T. (1986). *A Nation of Excellence*. Address at Alumni International Singapore, Ministry of Communications and Information, Singapore, 1 December.

(1989). *Session No. 1, Volume No. 54, Sitting No. 8, Parliament No. 7*. Singapore Parliament Reports, Singapore, 29 November.

Gomez, E. T. (2002). 'Political Business in Malaysia: Party Factionalism, Corporate Development, and Economic Crisis'. In *Political Business in East Asia*, E. T. Gomez (ed.). London: Routledge, pp. 82–114.

(2019). 'Business as Usual: Regime Change and GLCs in Malaysia', *New Mandala*, 12 March. www.newmandala.org/business-as-usual-regime-change-and-glcs-in-malaysia/.

Gomez, E. T. and J. Saravanamutta. (2013). *The New Economic Policy in Malaysia: Affirmative Action, Ethnic Inequalities and Social Justice*. Singapore: National University Press.

Gooch, L. (2012). 'Police Clash with Protesters Seeking Electoral Reforms', *New York Times*, 28 April. www.nytimes.com/2012/04/29/world/asia/malaysian-capital-braces-for-rally-by-democracy-activists.html.

Gramsci, A. (1971). *Selections from the Prison Notebooks of Antonio Gramsci*. Q. Hoare and G. Nowell Smith (eds.). London: Lawrence and Wishart.

Hamid, A. F. A. and C. H. C. M. Razali. (2015). 'The Changing Face of Political Islam in Malaysia in the Era of Najib Razak, 2009–3013', *SOJOURN: Journal of Southeast Asian Studies*, 30(2): 301–37.

Han, K. (2020a). 'Growing a Movement in Activism-Averse Singapore', *New Naratif*, 15 January. https://newnaratif.com/journalism/growing-a-movement-in-activism-averse-singapore/share/pybxr/59e55259f971b935b82107ff58b740ab/.

(2020b). 'The Limits of Singaporean Activism', *New Naratif*, 17 January. https://newnaratif.com/journalism/growing-a-movement-in-activism-averse-singapore/share/pybxr/59e55259f971b935b82107ff58b740ab/.

(2020c). 'Will Covid-19 Show Us the Importance of Civil Society?', *A Magazine Singapore*, 5 May. https://read-a.com/will-covid-19-show-us-the-importance-of-civil-society/.

Hansson, E., K. Hewison, and J. Glassman. (2020). 'Legacies of the Cold War in East and Southeast Asia: An Introduction', Special Issue, *Journal of Contemporary Asia*, 50(4): 493–510.

Hansson, E. and M. Weiss (eds.). (2018). *Political Participation in Asia: Defining and Deploying Political Space*. New York: Routledge.

Harrington, M. (2019). 'Lessons from 2018: The Year of Uncivil Society', *UnHerd*, 26 December. https://unherd.com/2019/12/three-cheers-for-2018-the-year-of-uncivil-society/.

Hassan, H. (2018). 'Malaysian PM Mahathir Says His Party Needs to Defend "Weak" Malay Community', *Straits Times*, 29 December. www.straitstimes.com/asia/se-asia/malaysian-pm-mahathir-says-his-party-needs-to-defend-weak-malay-community.

(2019). 'PAS Delegate Warns Malaysia Could Become "Second Singapore" if Malay Rights Sidelined', *Straits Times*, 17 July. www.straitstimes.com/asia/se-asia/pas-delegate-warns-malaysia-could-become-second-singapore-if-malay-rights-sidelined.

Hau, C. (2017). *Elites and Illustrados in Philippine Culture*. Quezon City: Ateneo de Manila University Press.

Hedman, E. E. (2006). *In the Name of Civil Society: From Free Election Movements to People Power in the Philippines*. Honolulu, HI: University of Hawai'i Press.

Heng, P. K. (1997). 'The New Economic Policy and the Chinese Community in Peninsula Malaysia', *The Developing Economies*, 35(3): 262–92.

Hew, W. W. (2020). 'Manufacturing Malay Unity and the Downfall of Pakatan Harapan', *New Mandala*, 8 June. www.newmandala.org/manufacturing-malay-unity-and-the-downfall-of-pakatan-harapan/.

Hewison, K. (1989). *Bankers and Bureaucrats: Capital and the Role of the State in Thailand*. New Haven, CT: Yale University Southeast Asian Studies.

(2006). 'Thailand: Boom, Bust and Recovery'. In *The Political Economy of Southeast Asia: Markets, Power, and Contestation*, G. Rodan (ed.). Melbourne: Oxford University Press, pp.74–108.

(2010). 'Thaksin Shinawatra and the Reshaping of Thai Politics', *Contemporary Politics*, 16(2): 119–33.

(2019). 'Reluctant Populists: Learning Populism in Thailand', *International Political Science Review*, 38(4): 426–40.

(2020). 'Thai Youth Protests Undercut Political Establishment', *East Asia Forum*, 27 December. www.eastasiaforum.org/2020/12/27/youth-protests-undercut-thailands-political-establishment/.

(2021). 'Crazy Rich Thais: Thailand's Capitalist Class, 1980–2019', *Journal of Contemporary Asia*, 51(2): 262–77.

Hewison, K. and K. Kengkij. (2010). '"Thai-Style Democracy": The Royalist Struggle for Thailand's Politics'. In *Saying the Unsayable: Monarchy and Democracy in Thailand*, S. Ivarsson and L. Isager (eds.). Copenhagen: Nordic Institute for Southeast Asian Studies Press, pp. 179–202.

Hewison, K. and G. Rodan. (1994). 'The Decline of the Left in Southeast Asia'. In *The Socialist Register 1994*, R. Miliband and L. Panitch (eds.). London: Merlin Press, pp. 235–62.

(2012). 'Southeast Asia: The Left and the Rise of Bourgeois Opposition'. In *Routledge Handbook of Southeast Asian Politics*, R. Robison (ed.). London: Routledge, pp. 25–39.

Hewison, K., G. Rodan, and R. Robison. (1993). 'Introduction: Changing Forms of State Power in Southeast Asia'. In *Southeast Asia in the 1990s: Authoritarianism, Democracy and Capitalism*, K. Hewison, R. Robison and G. Rodan (eds.). Sydney: Allen and Unwin, pp. 2–8.

Heydarian, R. (2020). 'Duterte's Threats Against Business are Driving Investment Away', *Nikkei Asia*, 4 March. https://asia.nikkei.com/Opinion/Duterte-s-threats-against-business-are-driving-investment-away.

Hicken, A. and E. Kuhonta (eds.). (2014). *Party System Institutionalization in Asia: Democracies, Autocracies, and the Shadows of the Past*. New York: Cambridge University Press.

Hicken, A. and E. M. Kuhonta (eds). 2015. *Party System Institutionalisation in Asia: Democracies, Autocracies and the Shadows of the Past*. New York: Cambridge University Press.

Hilley, J. (2001). *Malaysia: Mahathirism, Hegemony and the New Opposition*. London: Zed Books.

Huang, P. C. C. (1993). '"Public Sphere"/"Civil Society" in China?', *Modern China*, 19(2): 216–40.

Huntington, S. P. (1991). *The Third Wave: Democratization in the Late Twentieth Century*. Norman, OK: University of Oklahoma Press.

Hutchison, J. (2006). 'Poverty of Politics in the Philippines'. In *The Political Economy of South-East Asia: Conflicts, Crises and Change*, G. Rodan, K. Hewison, and R. Robison (eds.). Melbourne: Oxford University Press, pp. 42–70.

(2012). 'Labour Politics in Southeast Asia: The Philippines in Comparative Perspective'. In *Routledge Handbook of Southeast Asian Politics*, R. Robison (ed.). Abingdon: Routledge, pp. 40–52.

Hutchison, J. and A. Brown (eds.). (2001). *Organising Labour in Globalising Asia*. London: Routledge.

Janjira, S. (2018). 'Conservative Civil Society in Thailand'. In *The Mobilization of Conservative Civil Society*, R. Youngs (ed.). Washington D.C.: Carnegie Endowment for International Peace, pp. 27–32. https://carnegieendow ment.org/files/Youngs_Conservative_Civil_Society_

(2021). 'The Dark Side of Civil Society? How Thailand's Civic Networks Foster Autocracy', *Melbourne Asia Review*, 2 June. https://melbournea siareview.edu.au/the-dark-side-of-civil-society-how-thailands-civic-net works-foster-autocracy/.

Jayasuriya, K. (2020). 'The Rise of the Right: Populism and Authoritarianism in Southeast Asian Politics'. In *Southeast Asian Affairs 2020*, M.Cook and D. Singh (eds.) . Singapore: ISEAS, pp. 43–56.

Jayasuriya, K. and K. Hewison (2004). 'The Antipolitics of Good Governance: From Global Social Policy to a Global Populism?', *Critical Asian Studies*, 36(4): 571–90.

Jayasuriya, J. and G. Rodan. (2007). 'Beyond Hybrid Regimes: More Participation, Less Contestation in Southeast Asia', *Democratization*, 14(5): 773–94.

Jerusalem, P. (2018). 'Why the Pink Dot and LGBTIQ Movement in Singapore is Ready', *Outright*, 1 August. https://outrightinternational.org/content/ why-pink-dot-and-lgbtiq-movement-singapore-ready.

Jomo, K. S. (1994). *U-Turn? Malaysian Economic Development Policies after 1990*. Townsville: James Cook University.

Josey, A. (1974). *The Struggle for Singapore*. Sydney: Angus & Robertson.

Kanokwan, M. (2020). 'NGOs and Civil Society in Thailand'. In *Routledge Handbook of Contemporary Thailand*, C. Pavin (ed.). London: Routledge, pp. 306–78.

Kassim, Y. R. (2020). 'Malaysia's Epic Power Struggle', *East Asia Forum*, 25 March. www.eastasiaforum.org/2020/03/25/malaysias-epic-power-struggle/.

Kathiravelu, L. (2020). 'COVID-19 Exposes Singapore Migrant Worker Experience', *East Asia Forum*, 11 November. www.eastasiaforum.org/2020/11/11/covid-19-exposes-the-singapore-migrant-worker-experience/.

Keane, J. (1999). *Civil Society*. Stanford, CA: Stanford University Press.

(2005). 'Eleven Theses on Markets and Civil Society', *Journal of Civil Society*, 1(1): 25–34.

Kengkij, K. and K. Hewison. (2009). 'Social Movements and Political Opposition in Contemporary Thailand', *The Pacific Review*, 22(4): 451–77.

Kerkvleit, B. (1977). *The Huk Rebellion: A Study of Peasant Revolt in the Philippines*. Berkeley: University of California Press.

Khoo, B. T. (2006). 'Malaysia Balancing Development and Power'. In *The Political Economy of South-East Asia*, G. Rodan, K. Hewison, and R. Robison (eds.). Melbourne: Oxford University Press, pp. 170–96.

(2020). *Malay Politics: Parlous Condition, Continuing Problems*. Trends in Southeast Asia, Issue 17. Singapore: Institute of Southeast Asian Studies.

Khoo, Y. K. (2015). 'Malaysia's Bersih 5 Rally: Protesters Weigh the Cost of Action under a Repressive Regime', *The Conversation*, 18 November. https://theconversation.com/malaysias-bersih-5-rally-protesters-weigh-the-cost-of-action-under-a-repressive-regime-68723.

Kim, E. and J. Yoo. (2015). 'Conditional Cash Transfer in the Philippines: How to Overcome Institutional Constraints for Implementing Social Protection', *Asia and the Pacific Policy Studies*, 2(1): 75–89.

Kingston, J. (2020). 'Uncivil Society: Religious Organisations, Mobocracy and Democratic Backsliding in Asia', *Forces of Renewal in Southeast Asia (FORSEA)*, 7 August. https://forsea.co/uncivil-society-religious-organisations-mobocracy-and-democratic-backsliding-in-asia/.

Koh, C. Y., C. Goh, K. Wee, and B. S. A. Yeoh. (2017). 'Drivers of Migration Policy Reform: The Day Off Policy for Migrant Domestic Workers in Singapore', *Global Social Policy*, 17(2): 188–205.

Kopecký, P. and C. Mudde. (2003). 'Rethinking Civil Society'. *Democratisation*, 10(3): 1-14.

Kow, G. C. (2015). 'Bersih 4 will be a Show of No Confidence in Najib', *Malaysiakini*, 14 August. www.malaysiakini.com/news/308638.

Kunihara, K. K. (1945). *Labor in the Philippine Economy*. Stanford, CA: Stanford University Press.

Kurlantzick, J. (2020). 'Addressing the Effects of COVID-19 on Democracy in South and Southeast Asia', *Council on Foreign Relations*, November.

www.cfr.org/report/addressing-effect-covid-19-democracy-south-and-southeast-asia.

Laclau, E. (2007). *On Populist Reason*. London: Verso Books.

Laine, J. P. (2014). 'Debating Civil Society: Contested Conceptualizations and Development Trajectories', *International Journal of Not-for -Profit Law*, 16(1): 59–77.

Landau, I. (2008). 'Law and Civil Society in Cambodia and Vietnam: A Gramscian Perspective', *Journal of Contemporary Asia*, 38(2): 244–58.

Lane, M. R. (1990). *The Urban Mass Movement in the Philippines, 1983–87*. Singapore: Institute of Southeast Asian Studies.

Lee, H. G. (2008). 'Malaysia in 2007: Abdullah Administration under Siege'. In *Southeast Asian Affairs 2008*, D. Singh and T. M. M. Than (eds.). Singapore: Institute of Southeast Asian Affairs, pp. 188–206.

Lee, H. L. (1999). Speech delivered at the Administrative Services Dinner and Promotion Ceremony, Mandarin Hotel, Singapore, 29 March. www.singapore21.org.sg/speeches_290399.html.

(2013). Speech presented by Prime Minister Lee Hsien Loong at the People's Action Party Convention, 7 December. www.pap.org.sg/conference-convention/party-convention-2013-speech-by-pm-lee-hsien-loong/

Lee, L. T. (1999). 'NECC II to Consult All Segments of Society', *New Straits Times*, 16 August. www.nas.gov.sg/archivesonline/data/pdfdoc/1999032903.htm

Lee, T. (2005). 'Gestural Politics: Civil Society in "New" Singapore', *SOJOURN: Journal of Southeast Asian Studies*, 20(2): 132–54.

Lemiére, S. (2014). 'Gangsta and Politics in Malaysia'. In *Misplaced Democracy: Malaysian Politics and People*, S. Lemiére (ed.). Petalying Jaya: Strategic Information and Research Development Centre, pp. 91–108.

Levitsky, S. and L. A. Way. (2010). *Competitive Authoritarianism: Hybrid Regimes after the Cold War*. New York: Cambridge University Press.

Liew, C. T. (2013). 'An Opposition's Transformation: Interview with Liew Chin Tong'. In *Awakening: The Abdullah Years in Malaysia,* B. Welsh and J. Chin (eds.). Petaling Jaya: Strategic Information and Research Development Centre, pp. 294–311.

Lim, L. (2020). 'COVID-19's Implications for Singapore's Future Economy', *Academia SG*, 13 April. www.academia.sg/academic-views/covid-19s-implications-for-singapores-future-economy/.

Lorch, J. (2021). 'Elite Capture, Civil Society and Democratic Backsliding in Bangladesh, Thailand and the Philippines', *Democratization*, 28(1): 81–102.

Malaysiakini. (2019). '"Deep State" the Important Reason Why Reforms Slow', *Head Topics*, 30 July. https://headtopics.com/my/deep-state-the-important-reason-why-reforms-slow-7223285.

Mauzy, D. (1995). 'The Tentative Life and Quiet Death of the NECC in Malaysia'. In *Managing Change in Southeast Asia: Local Initiatives, Global Connections*, J. de Bernadi, G. Forth, and S. Niessen (eds.). Montreal: University of Montreal, pp. 77–92.

McCargo, D. and T. Naruemon. (2021). 'Plural Partisans: Thailand's People's Democratic Reform Committee Protesters', *Contemporary Southeast Asia*, 43(1): 125–50.

Meyer, P. (2020). 'Singapore's First Election under the New Fake News Law', *The Diplomat*, 7 July. https://thediplomat.com/2020/07/singapores-first-election-under-the-fake-news-law/.

Mietzner, M. (2021). *Democratic Deconsolidation in Southeast Asia*. Cambridge and New York: Cambridge University Press.

Mirsky, Y. (1993). 'Democratic Politics, Democratic Culture', *Orbis*, 37(4): 567–80.

Missingham, B. D. (2003). *The Assembly of the Poor in Thailand: From Local Struggles to National Protest Movement*. Bangkok: Silkworm Books.

Mohammad, M. 2009. 'Politics of the NEP and Ethnic Relations in Malaysia'. In *Multiethnic Malaysia: Past, Present and Future,* T. G. Lim, A. Gomes, and Azly Rahman (eds.). Petaling Jaya: Strategic Information and Research Development Centre, pp. 113–39.

Morgenbesser, L. (2019). *The Rise of Sophisticated Authoritarianism in Southeast Asia*. Cambridge and New York: Cambridge University Press.

Morlino, L., B. Dressel, and R. Pelizzo. (2011). 'The Quality of Democracy in Asia-Pacific: Issues and Findings', *International Political Science Review*, 32(5): 491–511.

Mouzelis, N. (1985). 'On the Concept of Populism: Populist and Clientelist Modes of Incorporation into Semiperipheral Polities', *Politics & Society*, 14(3): 329–48.

Munro-Kua, A. (1996). *Authoritarian Populism in Malaysia*. London: Macmillan.

New York Times (2006). 'In Singapore's Election, the Protest Vote Grows Louder'. 7 May. www.nytimes.com/2006/05/07/world/asia/07iht-sing.html

Ng, J. S. (2019). '377A Will Be Around "For Some Time," Will Not Inhibit How Singapore Attracts Tech Talent: PM Lee', *Today Online*, 27 June. www.todayonline.com/singapore/377a-will-be-around-some-time-will-not-inhibit-how-spore-attracts-tech-talent-pm-lee.

Ngiam, S. T. (2020). 'How Gerrymandering Creates Unfair Elections in Singapore', *New Naratif*, 2 April. https://newnaratif.com/research/how-gerrymandering-creates-unfair-elections-in-singapore/.

Nonini, D. M. (2015). *'Getting By': Class and State Formation Among Chinese in Malaysia*. Ithaca, NY: Cornell University Press.

Ong, K. M. (2011). 'Bersih 2.0 Rally in Malaysia Stirs Discontent with Ruling Party', *East Asia Forum*, 13 August. www.eastasiaforum.org/2011/08/13/bersih-2-0-rally-in-malaysia-stirs-discontent-with-ruling-party/.

Online Citizen. (2021). 'The Online Citizen Stands in Solidarity with Dr. Pj Thum and the New Naratif', 5 March. www.theonlinecitizen.com/2021/03/05/the-online-citizen-stands-in-solidarity-with-dr-pj-thum-and-the-new-naratif/.

Ortmann, S. (2015). 'Political Change and Civil Society Coalitions in Singapore', *Government and Opposition*, 50(1): 119–39.

O'Shannassy, M. (2008). 'Beyond the Barisan Nasional? A Gramscian Perspective of the 2008 Malaysian General Election', *Contemporary Southeast Asia*, 31(1): 88–109.

Paladino, B. (2018). 'Democracy Disconnected: Social Media's Caustic Influence on Southeast Asia's Fragile Republics', *Foreign Policy at Brookings,* July. www.brookings.edu/research/democracy-disconnected-social-medias-caustic-influence-on-southeast-asias-fragile-republics/.

Pasit, W. (2020). 'From "Being Thai" to "Being Human": Thailand's Protests and Redefining the Nation', *New Mandala*, 26 November. www.newmandala.org/thank-you-for-seeing-our-worth-amid-a-pandemic-redshirts-joined-thailands-youth-led-protests/.

Pasuk, P. and C. Baker. (2008). 'Introduction'. In *Thai Capital After the 1997 Crisis*, P. Pasuk and C. Baker (eds). Chiang Mai: Silkworm, pp. 1–16.

(2009). *Thaksin: The Business of Politics in Thailand*. Chiang Mai: Silkworm Books.

(2011). 'Populist Challenge to the Establishment: Thaksin Shinawatra and the Transformation of Thai Politics.' In *Routledge Handbook of Southeast Asian Politics*, R. Robison (ed.). Abingdon: Routledge, pp. 83–96.

Penchan, P. (2021). 'Thai Youth's Struggle for Democracy May Fizzle But Political Contention Continues,' *East Asia Forum*, 11 May. https://www.eastasiaforum.org/2021/05/11/thai-youths-struggle-for-democracy-may-fizzle-but-political-contention-continues/

Perimbanayagam, K. (2018). 'Gerakan Pembela Ummah Issues 10 Demands to Government', *New Straits Times*, 29 July. www.nst.com.my/news/politics/2018/07/395407/gerakan-pembela-ummah-issues-10-demands-government-nsttv.

Peterson, W. (2001). *Theater and the Politics of Culture in Contemporary Singapore*. Middletown, CT: Wesleyan University Press.

Philippine Statistics Authority. (2017). 'Total Number of OFWs Estimated at 2.2 Million (Results from the 2016 Survey on Overseas Filipinos)', Reference Number: 2017–043, 27 April. https://psa.gov.ph/content/total-number-ofws-estimated-22-million-results-2016-survey-overseas-filipinos.

Pitkin, H. F. (1967). *The Concept of Representation*. Berkeley, CA: University of California Press.

Platek, D. and P. Pluecienniczak. (2016). 'Civil Society and Extreme-Right Collective Action in Poland, 1990–2013', *Revue D'Etudes Comparatives Est-Quest*, 47: 117–46.

Porcalla, D. (2013). 'Code-NGO Gets P8 M from Palace', *The Philippine Star*, 15 October. www.philstar.com/headlines/2013/10/15/1245424/code-ngo-gets-p8-m-palace.

Prajak, K. (2016). 'Thailand's Failed 2014 Election: The Anti-Election Movement, Violence and Democratic Breakdown', *Journal of Contemporary Asia*, 46(3): 467–85.

Puthucheary, J. (1960). *Ownership and Control of the Malaysian Economy*. Singapore: Eastern University Press.

Putnam, R. D. (1993). *Making Democracy Work: Civic Traditions in Modern Italy*. New Jersey: Princeton University Press.

(1995). 'Bowling Alone: America's Declining Social Capital'. *Journal of Democracy*, 6(1): 65–78.

(2000). *Bowling Alone: The Collapse and Revival of American Community*. New York: Simon & Schuster.

Pye, O. and W. Schaffar. (2008). 'The 2006 Anti-Thaksin Movement in Thailand: An Analysis', *Journal of Contemporary Asia*, 38(1): 38–61.

Quimpo, N. G. (2008). *Contested Democracy and the Left in the Philippines after Marcos*. New Haven, CT: Yale University Press.

Rappler. (2017). 'Fast Facts: What is the PCOO?', 12 May. www.rappler.com/newsbreak/iq/fast-facts-presidential-communications-operations-office-pcoo.

Raquiza, A. (2014). 'Changing Configuration of Philippine Capitalism'. *Philippine Political Science Journal*, 35(2): 225–50.

Ratcliffe, R. (2020). 'Philippines War on Drugs May Have Killed Tens of Thousands, Says UN', *The Guardian*, 4 June. www.theguardian.com/world/2020/jun/04/philippines-police-may-have-killed-tens-of-thousands-with-near-impunity-in-drug-war-un.

Reid, B. (2005). 'Poverty Alleviation and Participatory Development in the Philippines', *Journal of Contemporary Asia*, 35(1): 29–52.

(2008). 'Developmental NGOs, Semiclientelism, and the State in the Philippines: From "Crossover" to Double-crossed', *Kasarinlan: Philippine Journal of Third World Studies*, 23(1): 4–42.

Rodan, G. (1989). *The Political Economy of Singapore's Industrialization*. London: Macmillan.

(1997). 'Civil Society and Other Possibilities in Southeast Asia', *Journal of Contemporary Asia*, 27(2): 156–78.

(2004). *Transparency and Authoritarian Rule: Singapore and Malaysia*. London: RoutledgeCurzon.

(2016). 'Capitalism, Inequality and Ideology in Singapore: New Challenges for the Ruling Party', *Asian Studies Review*, 40(2): 211–30.

(2018). *Participation without Democracy: Containing Conflict in Southeast Asia*. Ithaca, NY: Cornell University Press.

(2020). 'Early Election Backfires on Singapore Ruling Party', *East Asia Forum*, 20 July. www.eastasiaforum.org/2020/07/20/early-election-back fires-on-singapores-ruling-party/.

Rodan, G. and C. Hughes. (2014). *The Politics of Accountability in Southeast Asia: The Dominance of Moral Ideologies*. Oxford: Oxford University Press.

Rodan, G. and K. Jayasuriya. (2007). 'The Technocratic Politics of Administrative Participation: Case Studies of Singapore and Vietnam', *Democratization*, 14(5): 795–815.

Rosenblum, N. L. (2000). 'Primus Inter Pares: Political Parties and Civil Society', *Chicago-Kent Law Review*, 75(2): 493–529.

Rueschemeyer D., E. H. Stephens, and J. D. Stephens. (1992). *Capitalist Development and Democracy*. Chicago: Chicago University Press.

Ruzza, C. (2009). 'Populism and Euroscepticism: Towards Uncivil Society?', *Policy and Society*, 28: 87–98.

Sanchez, E. M. and J. S. Lamchek. (2021). 'The Year of Daring: Revisiting the Philippine Left's Dalliance with a Strongman', 6th ed., *Melbourne Asia Review*, 10 May. https://melbourneasiareview.edu.au/the-year-of-daring-revisiting-the-philippine-lefts-dalliance-with-a-strongman/.

Saowanee, T. A. (2021). '"Thank You for Seeing Our Worth": Amid a Pandemic, Redshirts Joined Thailand's Youth-Led Protests', *New Mandala*, 2 April. www.newmandala.org/thank-you-for-seeing-our worth-amid-a-pandemic-redshirts-joined-thailands-youth-led-protests/.

Seah, C. M. (1973). *Community Centres in Singapore*. Singapore: Singapore University Press.

Searle, P. (1999). *The Riddle of Malaysian Capitalism: Rent Seekers or Real Capitalists?* Honolulu: Australian Association of Asian Studies in association with Allen & Unwin and University of Hawaii Press.

Seow, F. (1998). *The Media Enthralled: Singapore Revisited.* Boulder, CO: Lynne Rienner.

Sidel, J. T. (1999). *Capital, Coercion and Crime: Bossism in the Philippines.* Stanford, CA: Stanford University Press.

Sinpeng, A. (2021). *Opposing Democracy in the Digital Age: The Yellow Shirts in Thailand.* Ann Arbor, MI: University of Michigan Press.

Skocpol, T. (2004). *Diminished Democracy: From Membership to Management in American Civil Life.* Norman, OK: University of Oklahoma Press.

Slater, D. (2015). 'Malaysia's Mess is Mahathir-Made', *East Asia Forum*, 29 July. www.eastasiaforum.org/2015/07/29/malaysias-mess-is-mahathir-made/.

Solomon, F. (2016). 'Thailand is Marking the Darkest Day in its Living Memory', *Time*, 6 October. https://time.com/4519367/thailand-bangkok-october-6-1976-thammasat-massacre-students-joshua-wong/.

Somchai, P. (2016). 'Rural Transformations and Democracy in Northeast Thailand', *Journal of Contemporary Asia*, 46(3): 134–49.

Soon, C. and G. Koh. (2017). 'Introduction'. In *Civil Society and the State in Singapore*, C. Soon and G. Koh (eds.). London: World Scientific, pp. xi–xliii.

Sopranzetti, C. (2020). 'Mass Politics and the Red Shirts'. In *Routledge Handbook of Contemporary Thailand*, C. Pavin (ed.). London: Routledge, pp. 156–62.

Stid, D. (2018). 'Civil Society and the Foundations of Democratic Citizenship', *Stanford Social Innovation Review*, 16 August. https://ssir.org/articles/entry/civil_society_and_the_foundations_of_democratic_citizenship.

Straits Times Weekly Overseas Edition (STWOE). (1989). 'Nothing to Lose from Having Nominated MPs, Says BG Lee', 9 December.

Tan, K. P. (2012). 'The Ideology of Pragmatism: Neo-Liberal Globalisation and Political Authoritarianism in Singapore', *Journal of Contemporary Asia*, 42(1): 67–92.

Tan, K. Y. L. (2017). 'Growing Civil Society in Singapore: The Future Legislative Landscape'. In *Civil Society and the State in Singapore*, C. Soon and G. Koh (eds.). London: World Scientific, pp. 241–80.

Tan, N. (2020). 'Minimal Factionalism in Singapore's People's Action Party', *Journal of Current Southeast Asian Affairs*, 39(1): 124–43.

Tan, N. and B. Grofman. (2018). 'Electoral Rules and Manufacturing Legislative Supermajority: Evidence from Singapore', *Commonwealth & Comparative Politics*, 56(3): 273–97.

Tawatao, D. (2014). 'Is Catholic Church's Influence in Philippines Fading?', *BBC News*, 25 May. www.bbc.com/news/world-asia-27537943.

Tay, D. (1999), 'Opposition Should Forget Differences'. *New Straits Times*, 12 August.

Taylor, M. (2020). 'Retired Doctor Launches New Legal Bid to End Singapore's Gay Ban', *Reuters*, 4 December. www.reuters.com/article/us-singapore-lgbt-court-trfn-idUSKBN28E12Z.

Teo, T.-A. (2019). 'Perceptions of Meritocracy in Singapore: Inconsistencies, Contestations and Biases', *Asian Studies Review*, 43(2): 184–205.

Teoh, S. (2015). '"Red Shirt" Rally Brings Out Malaysians' Insecurities', *Straits Times*, 30 September. www.asiaone.com/red-shirt-rally-brings-out-malaysians-insecurities?amp.

Thanasak, J. and A. Gethin. (2019). 'Extreme Inequality, Democratisation and Class Struggle in Thailand', Issue Brief 2019-1, *World Inequality Lab*, 24 March. https://wid.world/document/extreme-inequality-democratisation-and-class-struggles-in-thailand-wid-world-issuebrief-2019-1/.

The Star. (2019). 'Malaysia Withdraws from the Rome Statute', 5 April. www.thestar.com.my/news/nation/2019/04/05/malaysia-withdraws-from-ther ome-statute/.

Thompson, M. R. (2016). 'Bloodied Democracy: Duterte and the Death of Liberal Reformism in the Philippines', *Journal of Current Southeast Asian Affairs*, 35(3): 39–68.

(2021). 'Are Duterte's Political Fortunes Term-Limited?', *East Asia Forum*, 25 April. www.eastasiaforum.org/2021/04/25/are-dutertes-political-for tunes-term-limited/.

Thorn, P. (2017). 'Redefining Democratic Discourse in Thailand's Civil Society'. In *Military, Monarchy and Repression: Assessing Thailand's Authoritarian Turn*, K. Veerayooth and K. Hewison (eds.). London: Routledge, pp. 150–67.

Timberman, D. G. (2019). *Philippine Politics under Duterte: A Midterm Assessment*. Washington, DC: Carnegie Endowment for International Peace. https://carnegieendowment.org/2019/01/10/philippine-politics-under-duterte-midterm-assessment-pub-78091.

Toepler, S., A. Zimmer, C. Frölich, and K. Obuch. (2020). 'The Changing Space for NGOs: Civil Society in Authoritarian and Hybrid Regimes', *Voluntas*, 31: 649–62.

Törnquist, O. (2013). 'Democracy and the Philippine Left'. In *Introduction to Philippine Politics: Local Politics and State Building and Democratization*, M. E. Atienza (ed.). Quezon City: University of the Philippines Press, pp. 170–219.

Tremewan, C. (1994). *The Political Economy of Social Control in Singapore.* London: Macmillan Press.

Tsun, H. T. (2010). 'Malaysia's Electoral System: Government of the People?', *Asian Journal of Comparative Law*, 5(1): 1–32.

Ukrist, P. and M. K. Connors. (2021). 'Thailand's Public Secret: Military Wealth', *Journal of Contemporary Asia*, 51(2): 278–302.

United Nations Development Program (UNDP). (2014). *Malaysia Human Development Report 2013: Redesigning an Inclusive Future.* Kuala Lumpur: United Nations Development Program.

Veerayooth, K. (2018a). 'Contingent Authoritarians: Why Thai Civil Society and the Middle Class Oppose Democracy'. In *Middle Class, Civil Society and Democracy in Asia*, H. M. Hsao (ed.). London: Routledge, pp. 149–70.

(2018b). 'Thailand Trapped: Catch-Up Legacies and Contemporary Malaise', *TRaNS: Trans-Regional and-National Studies of Southeast Asia*, 6(2): 253–77.

Viterna, J., E. Clough, and K. Clarke. (2015). 'Reclaiming the "Third Sector" from "Civil Society": A New Agenda for Development Studies', *Sociology of Development*, 1(1): 173–207.

Waldner, D. and E. Lust. (2018). 'Unwelcome Change: Coming to Terms with Democratic Backsliding', *Annual Review of Political Science*, 21: 93–113.

Walzer, M. (1991). 'The Idea of Civil Society', *Dissent*, 38(2): 293–304.

Weiss, M. L. (2006). *Protest and Possibilities: Civil Society and Coalitions for Political Change in Malaysia.* Stanford, CA: Stanford University Press.

(2014). 'Of Inequality and Irritation: New Agendas and Activism in Malaysia and Singapore', *Democratization*, 21(5): 867–87.

(2020). *The Roots of Resilience: Party Machines and Grassroots Politics in Southeast Asia.* Ithaca, NY: Cornell University Press.

(2021). 'Can Civil Society Safeguard Rights in Asia?', *Asian Studies Review*, 45(1): 13–27.

Welsh, B. (2013). 'Malaysia's Elections: A Step Backward', *Journal of Democracy*, 24(3): 18–32.

(2018). '*Hanta Raya*: UMNO's Dead End Politics'. In *The End of UMNO? Essays on Malaysia's Former Dominant Party*, B. Welsh (ed.). Petaling Jaya: Strategic Information and Development Research Centre, pp. 345–80.

Wilson, I. (2019). 'Between Throwing Rocks and a Hard Place: FPI and the Jakarta Riots', *New Mandala*, 2 June. www.newmandala.org/between-throwing-rocks-and-a-hard-place-fpi-and-the-jakarta-riots/.

Wolters, W. (1984). *Politics, Patronage and Class Conflict in Central Luzon.* Quezon City: New Day Publishers.

Wong, C. H. and N. Othman. (2009). 'Malaysia at 50: An "Electoral One-Party State"? In *Governing Malaysia*, A. R. Baginda (ed.). Kuala Lumpur: Malaysia Strategic Research Centre, pp. 1–58.

Wood, E. M. (1990). 'The Uses and Abuses of "Civil Society"'. In *Socialist Register 1990*, R. Miliband, L. Panitch, and J. Saville (eds.). London: Merlin Press, pp. 60–84.

Wurfel, D. (1959). 'Unions and Labor Policy in the Philippines', *Industrial and Labor Relations Review*, 12(4): 582–608.

Youngs, R. (ed.). (2018). *The Mobilization of Conservative Civil Society*. Washington D.C.: Carnegie Endowment for International Peace, pp. 27–32. https://carnegieendowment.org/files/Youngs_Conservative_Civil_Society_FINAL.pdf.

Acknowledgements

Many thanks to three anonymous reviewers for their constructive criticisms and suggestions, and to Kanishka Jayasuriya, Kevin Hewison, Jane Hutchison, and Richard Robison for valuable feedback at different points in this project. I am also grateful to Meredith Weiss and Edward Aspinall for the opportunity to contribute to this series and for their expert advice during the review process.

Cambridge Elements ≡

Politics and Society in Southeast Asia

Edward Aspinall

Australian National University

Edward Aspinall is a professor of politics at the Coral Bell School of Asia-Pacific Affairs, Australian National University. A specialist of Southeast Asia, especially Indonesia, much of his research has focused on democratisation, ethnic politics and civil society in Indonesia and, most recently, clientelism across Southeast Asia.

Meredith L. Weiss

University at Albany, SUNY

Meredith L. Weiss is Professor of Political Science at the University at Albany, SUNY. Her research addresses political mobilization and contention, the politics of identity and development, and electoral politics in Southeast Asia, with particular focus on Malaysia and Singapore.

About the Series

The Elements series Politics and Society in Southeast Asia includes both country-specific and thematic studies on one of the world's most dynamic regions. Each title, written by a leading scholar of that country or theme, combines a succinct, comprehensive, up-to-date overview of debates in the scholarly literature with original analysis and a clear argument.

Cambridge Elements ≡

Politics and Society in Southeast Asia

Printed in the United States
by Baker & Taylor Publisher Services